I AM

WH ... ... I AM

I HAVE

WHAT THE BIBLE SAYS I HAVE

I CAN

DO WHAT THE BIBLE SAYS I CAN DO

JAKE & KEITH PROVANCE

WORD & SPIRIT
PUBLISHING

I Am What The Bible Says I Am
I Have What The Bible Says I Have
I Can Do What The Bible Says I Can Do
ISBN: 978-1-949106-61-9
Copyright © 2021 by Word and Spirit Publishing

Published by Word and Spirit Publishing
P.O. Box 701403
Tulsa, Oklahoma 74170

Introduction

The Bible tells us that when we accept the Lord as our personal Savior, a spiritual metamorphosis takes place. We become new creatures in Christ, authorized by our union with Christ and empowered by the Holy Spirit to live as victors and overcomers in this life. Most Christians live far below the rights and privileges afforded to them. It is God's will and desire for us to live our life as victors and not as victims. In order to do this, it is essential that we become students of His Word. This is where our faith to live the life that Jesus died for us to live begins. This is where the will of God becomes known to you. God has specifically laid out in His Word who we are *in Christ,* what we have because of Christ, and what we can do *through Christ*. By learning these truths, we begin our victorious journey, and by meditating on them daily, these truths become more real to us than the problems we experience in this life.

The Bible is God's love letter to you, His child, telling you how to develop a personal and intimate relationship with Him. It is an instruction manual, a guidebook, and a road map filled with wisdom, insights, and guidance on how to navigate through this life. Through His Word, you can experience His love, joy, and peace on a daily basis and fulfill His plan and purpose for your life.

Three of the greatest spiritual realities that every believer should identify and assimilate into their walk with Christ as they read and study God's Word include:

> What the Bible says about our identity as born-again, new creatures in Christ

> What we have received through the redemptive work of Christ

> What we can do as Christians who are empowered by the Holy Spirit

We encourage and challenge you to meditate on these truths, mark them in your own Bible, pray them, and declare them over your life. Ask the Holy Spirit to help you walk in the light and revelation of these truths.

Our hope and prayer for you is the same as the apostle Paul, who prayed this prayer for believers recorded in the book of Ephesians:

For I always pray to the God of our Lord Jesus Christ, the Father of glory, that He may grant you a spirit of wisdom and revelation of insight into mysteries and secrets in the deep and intimate knowledge of Him, by having the eyes of your heart flooded with light, so that you can know and understand the hope to which He has called you, and how rich is His glorious inheritance in the saints (His set-apart ones), and so that you can know and understand what is the immeasurable and unlimited and surpassing greatness of His power in and for us who believe, as demonstrated in the working of His mighty strength (Ephesians 1:17–19 AMPC).

Contents

I CAN DO WHAT THE BIBLE SAYS I CAN DO

I AM

WHAT THE BIBLE SAYS I AM

Introduction

Who do you see when you look in the mirror? *Are you good looking? Are you smart? Are you kind? Are you strong? Are you valuable?*

Before you answer, take a moment to think about where your response is coming from. Why do you think these things about yourself? Where did they originate? Have they been spoken to you? Have you pondered them in your secret thoughts? Are they rooted in doubt and insecurity or in confidence and truth?

Too often we tend to conform to the opinions of those around us, and use comparison to build our self-worth. This is a sure recipe for disaster, for it leads to a very fickle, unhappy life. Comparison is a double-edged sword—too often leading to destruction. The stress of trying to fit in, wanting to stand out, the pressure to be perfect, etc., are all self-induced afflictions that rob us of our daily joy, peace, and contentment. That's why the Bible warns us, "But when they measure themselves by one another and compare themselves with one another, they are without understanding" (2 Corinthians 10:12 ESV).

But what if you could base your identity and self-worth on something besides the opinions of those around you or even your own opinions? What if your value was based on something that never changes? Something that is fixed and decided for all eternity—never to be undone? Whether you are a new believer or have been a Christian for many years, it is always important to be reminded of who God says you are. This book is a collection of those truths, to remind you and encourage you to stand tall in the reality of the "new you."

God never changes in His thoughts towards you. He does not look at you as a lump sum of your decisions, nor does He judge you based on your worthiness. The moment you surrender to God by believing in Him, and confessing Him as your Lord and Savior, is the moment God places a new identity on you and in you! He sees you as His child, He delights in your happiness, and it is

His firm desire to encourage and affirm your true identity—if you will let Him.

The Word of God is a living book full of life, love, and light. When you read God's words and speak them with faith, their power will take root in your heart, and infiltrate and permeate your mind. The full realization of who you are according to God may not happen overnight, but as you meditate and speak His words, the way you see yourself will begin to mesh with the way God sees you, and you'll be able to see those around you the way God sees them. You will never be the same!

I Am New

You became a new creation when you accepted Jesus as your personal Savior. You experienced the greatest miracle of God's Kingdom—a spiritual metamorphosis. One Bible translation says that you became a new species of being. God has forgiven the sins, mistakes, failures, and short-comings of your past, never to be remembered again. You may have some of the same thoughts, attitudes, and addictions, and you may even want to do some of the same old stuff, but don't get discouraged. Though Christ made your spirit new, *you* are the one who makes your mind new.

The Bible says to "put on the new you." This means it's a conscious choice to behave like and adopt the attitude of a new person in Christ. Choosing to do what is right, reading and listening to the Word of God, and praying are all part of becoming the new you. It doesn't happen completely overnight, but the moment you start to adapt your lifestyle is the moment your life begins to change! As you stick with it, you will begin to prefer God's way instead of your old ways of doing things.

How cool is it that with God you can actually change the way you think?! As you embrace the new you and renew your mind by reading, contemplating, and speaking His Word, you'll grow more and more aware of God's presence in your life. You'll notice with each passing day that your desires and thoughts are becoming more and more like His. You are *new* on the inside—believe and confess this over yourself daily, and watch your thoughts and actions change to reflect what is already yours.

Scriptures

"Therefore if any man be in Christ, he is a new creature: old things are passed away; behold, all things are become new."

–2 CORINTHIANS 5:17 (KJV)

"Remember not the former things, nor consider the things of old. Behold, I am doing a new thing; now it springs forth, do you not perceive it? I will make a way in the wilderness and rivers in the desert."

–ISAIAH 43:18-19 (ESV)

"Don't lie to each other, for you have stripped off your old sinful nature and all its wicked deeds. Put on your new nature, and be renewed as you learn to know your Creator and become like him."

–COLOSSIANS 3:9-10 (NLT)

"And I will give you a new heart, and I will put a new spirit in you. I will take out your stony, stubborn heart and give you a tender, responsive heart."

–EZEKIEL 36:26 (NLT)

Speak these words over your life

I am a new creation in Christ. All of my sins have been forgiven and forgotten. My old life and everything associated with it has passed away. I have new desires pleasing to God, and new goals for a life of peace, prosperity, and joy. I am committed to living a life of honor and integrity. I am committed to let God's love and light shine through me, and His wisdom guide me, change me, and mold me into what He desires I become. The old me is dead, there is a new person living on the inside of me. The Spirit of the Lord now lives in me and my mind will focus on those things that are pure. I am a new creation in Christ and His life within me will be evident for all to see.

I Am Free

Where the Spirit of the Lord is, there is *freedom*! When you accepted Jesus as your Savior, the supernatural-powered, bondage-breaking, addiction-killing Spirit of Freedom was infused into your very being. You are *free*! You no longer have to be chained up by the guilt of your past, for sin has lost its power over you and you have been forgiven.

You no longer have to be paralyzed by fear, for God will never leave you or forsake you. You no longer have to be a slave to your own lusts and desires, for there is a new force at work within you to equip, energize, and empower you. You no longer have to be confined by sickness and disease, for Christ made healing, wellness, and wholeness available for you. You no longer have to be plagued by the nagging thoughts of worry and anxiety, for God's ability to intervene is great, and greater still is His affection for you! You no longer have to be tortured by the need for others' approval, for you are a child of God, and He affirms you through His Word.

Satan's attacks against you are futile; God is with you, for you, and on your side! You are free to live the life you have always dreamed about. Nothing is too big or too far out of reach to an unshackled champion of God the Almighty. Jesus died on the cross to give you complete and total freedom, for nothing can halt the unstoppable life-altering force that is God's fierce love for those whose faith is audacious enough to believe in a loving God! YOU ARE FREE!

Scripture

"With the arrival of Jesus, the Messiah, that fateful dilemma is resolved. Those who enter into Christ's being-here-for-us no longer have to live under a continuous, low-lying black cloud. A new power is in operation. The Spirit of life in Christ, like a strong wind, has magnificently cleared the air, freeing you from a fated lifetime of brutal tyranny at the hands of sin and death."

–ROMANS 8:1-2 (MSG)

"In [this] freedom Christ has made us free [and completely liberated us]; stand fast then, and do not be hampered and held ensnared and submit again to a yoke of slavery [which you have once put off]."

–GALATIANS 5:1 (AMPC)

"So if the Son liberates you [makes you free men], then you are really and unquestionably free."

–JOHN 8:36 (AMPC)

Speak these words over your life

I am free. I am free from the guilt and condemnation of my past failures, for I have been forgiven. I am free from worry, anxiety, and stress, for the peace of God reigns in my heart. I am free from depression, discouragement, and despair, for the Lord encourages me and sustains me. I am free from fear, for God has not given me a spirit of fear, but of power, love, and a sound mind. I am free from addictions and the pull of my lusts and desires, for there is a new force at work within me to equip, energize, and empower me to live a life of honor. I am free from sickness and disease, for when Jesus took stripes on His back, He obliterated any power that sickness and disease had over me. I am free to live the life I have always dreamed about. Nothing is too big or too far out of reach to me—an unshackled champion of God the Almighty!

I Am Strong

Sometimes life can just wear you out! Weariness and fatigue always seem to be nipping at our heels. It's not just physical—the mental and emotional demands of life zap our strength and drain our energy. Our fast-paced lives are sometimes not conducive to the stress-free, worry-free, easy life we all seem to be chasing after. But don't lose heart! Look to God, and He will infuse strength into you, enabling you to not only endure the ever-constant pressures of life, but actually overcome them with joy!

The foundation and supplier of strength is the unfaltering Word of God. Reading, spending time thinking about, and speaking God's Word will allow His strength to flow to you. When you need strength to rise above all the negative words that people have spoken to you and about you, then remind yourself who God said you are and what He said you can do with Him. When you need strength to push through in the tough times, God will be your strength and walk through it with you. When you need strength in the mornings to face the grind, God is up with you to fight for you. When you need strength to get through depression, worry, or anxiety, then lean on God and He'll lift you up out of despair.

God is easily touched by what we are going through, and He never misses a chance to show Himself strong on behalf of those who love Him and put their trust in Him. When you need strength to overcome fear and your own insecurities, let God's strength bolster your heart with courage and confidence so you can face any circumstance head-on.

Scriptures

"In conclusion, be strong in the Lord [draw your strength from Him and be empowered through your union with Him] and in the power of His [boundless] might."

–EPHESIANS 6:10 (AMP)

"I can do all things [which He has called me to do] through Him who strengthens and empowers me [to fulfill His purpose—I am self-sufficient in Christ's sufficiency; I am ready for anything and equal to anything through Him who infuses me with inner strength and confident peace.]"

–PHILIPPIANS 4:13 (AMP)

"Have I not commanded you? Be strong and courageous. Do not be frightened, and do not be dismayed, for the Lord your God is with you wherever you go."

–JOSHUA 1:9 (ESV)

Speak these words over your life

I am strong in the Lord and in the power of His might. I am strong in my body. I am strong in my mind. I am strong in my spirit. I draw my strength through my union with Christ. When I am at my weakest, He is at His strongest. I can do all things through Him who strengthens and empowers me to fulfill His purpose. I am self-sufficient in Christ's sufficiency—I am ready for anything and equal to anything through Him who infuses me with inner strength and confident peace. I have strength to overcome any obstacle, to endure any attack, and to boldly fight the good fight of faith. I will not fear, nor will I allow any doubt to enter my mind, for I am a child of the Almighty and I will not be shaken! I am strong in the Lord!

I Am a Light in the Darkness

Darkness is all around us, seeking to dim our passion, hide our hope, and invade our peace. Christ has made you to be an example in this world—He wants His love and life to shine through you into the hearts of those around you. You are a light in the darkness!

Darkness takes many forms in people's lives. When we are depressed, it takes the form of heaviness; when we are angry, it clouds our judgement; when we are hurt, it feels cold and lonely. Darkness seeks to isolate us using depression, hate, confusion, and fear so we will push people away, develop addictions, and focus on our own inadequacies. But God has made us lights to pull people out of the darkness that envelops them. The only way to combat the darkness is to make the conscious choice to let God's light shine through you.

You can truly be a beacon of God's light, life, and love to a lost and dying world. Your life touches a great number of people every day. You can bring His life to the darkness in the lives around you. A smile, a kind word, a thoughtful gesture, a considerate response, a sympathetic ear, or a small act of kindness could have a significant effect on someone's life. His light in you can bring hope to the discouraged and heartbroken, healing to the sick and hurting, peace to a troubled mind, joy to the weary and distressed, and direction to those who have lost their way. Don't settle to live a life blending in; remember that you are a light in this world, a beacon of hope to those around you. Now, go and be that light in the darkness!

Scriptures

"You are the light of the world. You cannot hide a city that is on a mountain. Men do not light a lamp and put it under a basket. They put it on a table so it gives light to all in the house. Let your light shine in front of men. Then they will see the good things you do and will honor your Father Who is in heaven."

–MATTHEW 5:14-16 (NLV)

"You were once darkness, but now you are light in the Lord, so live your life as children of light."

–EPHESIANS 5:8 (CEB)

"Then Jesus again spoke to them, saying, "I am the Light of the world; he who follows Me will not walk in the darkness, but will have the Light of life."

–JOHN 8:12 (NASB)

Speak these words over your life

I am light in the darkness, a beacon of hope to all who see me. I will not settle for a life spent cowering in the shadows, afraid to allow the Light inside me to shine. I will make a difference in this world for the glory of God. Though sickness, sin, and suffering are all around me, they shall by no means affect me in any way, shape, or form. I operate on delegated authority from God the Almighty, and I refuse to allow evil in any form to live on in my spheres of influence. Goodness and mercy shall follow me wherever I go, for God is within me. Where there is a need, God will fulfill it through me. Where there is hurt, God will provide comfort through me. I proclaim that your Light, Father, shines through me more brightly every day.

I Am an Overcomer

This world can be a tough place. Jesus said that in the world we will have tribulation *and* distress *and* suffering, but to be courageous, be confident, be undaunted, and be filled with joy, for He has overcome the world. His conquest is accomplished, His victory abiding. You are an overcomer—God has decreed it through His Word, and it is an established fact. All you have to do is believe, receive, and act on it. The same life-giving, reality-shaping Spirit that raised Christ from the dead, overcoming even death, resides in you!

It is not the will of our Father to see you defeated by a problem, discouraged by an obstacle, or stressed by pressure. It's His firm desire that you choose life, that you choose to activate His gifts, that you choose to operate in faith, and that you live the joyfully fulfilled life of an overcomer.

So how do you overcome? By faith in God's Word. Your faith to overcome is not based on how you feel, and it's not conditional on how good you are. It's an unwavering trust that no matter how insurmountable an obstacle looks, your God will see you through to the other side of it. Take the dare to trust God above all things and to trust that with Him there is nothing you can't overcome. In the midst of the most daunting of challenges, dare to overcome. When faced with impossible odds, dare to overcome. When hope seems lost, dare to overcome! Pray to God, ask for help, find what His Word says about your situation, and then let God's Word guide your thoughts, words, and actions. By doing this, you are stepping into the identity of an overcomer.

Scriptures

"For everyone born of God is victorious *and* overcomes the world; and this is the victory that has conquered *and* overcome the world—our [continuing, persistent] faith [in Jesus the Son of God]. Who is the one who is victorious *and* overcomes the world? It is the one who believes *and* recognizes the fact that Jesus is the Son of God."

–1 John 5:4-5 (AMP)

"I have told you these things, so that in Me you may have [perfect] peace. In the world you have tribulation *and* distress *and* suffering, but be courageous [be confident, be undaunted, be filled with joy]; I have overcome the world." [My conquest is accomplished, My victory abiding.]"

–John 16:33 (AMP)

"He who overcomes [the world by adhering faithfully to Christ Jesus as Lord and Savior] will inherit these things, and I will be his God and he will be My son."

–Revelation 21:7 (AMP)

Speak these words over your life

I am an overcomer, strong in the Lord and the power of His might. I am confident, courageous, and undaunted in my faith. Even when I experience tribulation, tests, and trials, I shall overcome. I will not succumb to distress, frustration, or defeat. I am born of God and that makes me a world-overcomer. The same Spirit that raised Christ from the dead lives in me. I have been designed by God to succeed in this life. Through Him I can overcome any obstacle or challenge I might face. In spite of adverse circumstances and regardless of the failures of the past, even when faced with what seems to be impossible situations—I will still overcome by the power of the Holy Spirit. I will never give up; I will fight until I win. The battle is the Lord's and the victory is mine. I am an overcomer!

I Am a Child of God

Why does God treat us so lovingly when we sin constantly, spend our days ignoring Him at every turn, and only come to Him when we need something or a crisis happens in our life? Why would He send His only beloved Son, Jesus, to die a brutal death to save mankind after all of the crimes we have committed against Him (and still commit)? It makes no sense why God would do all of this for us unless there was an underlying reason for all of it. We may never be able to grasp the depth of His unconditional love for us, but God makes it clear why we are here—it's because He wanted to have children. He didn't want a servant, an employee, or a subject—He wanted a son or a daughter.

Have you ever wondered why you were born?

He wanted *you*.

You are His child; even when you mess up, you are still His. It brings joy to your Father when you are happy, when you succeed, and especially when you spend time with Him! He wants to be close to you and walk through life with you. All of the "rules" of the Bible are not set up so you can prove your love and devotion; they are there to protect you and help you live the most fulfilling life possible. Everything God has done has been out of His love for you. That's why He sent the dearest thing to His heart, Jesus, to die for you. He did it to show you just how valuable you are to Him and so He can spend eternity with you. You're His child, and heaven wouldn't be the same without you.

Scriptures

"And, I will be a Father to you, and you will be my sons and daughters, says the Lord Almighty."

–2 CORINTHIANS 6:18 (NIV)

"See how very much our Father loves us, for he calls us his children, and that is what we are! But the people who belong to this world don't recognize that we are God's children because they don't know him."

–1 JOHN 3:1 (NLT)

"For you [who are born-again have been reborn from above—spiritually transformed, renewed, sanctified and] are all children of God [set apart for His purpose with full rights and privileges] through faith in Christ Jesus."

–GALATIANS 3:26 (AMP)

Speak these words over your life

I am a child of the Almighty, with all the rights, privileges, and blessings that go with that position. The Creator of the universe is my Father. He loves me unconditionally. He wants me to succeed. He provides for all my needs. He's got my back, He is on my side. He forgives me when I mess up. He watches over me. He cares about what I care about. It gives Him pleasure to see me enjoying life, to see me succeeding, to see me trusting in Him despite any hardship this life throws at me. He sustains me; He sent His spirit to comfort and guide me. I am His child. He is my Father. There is not a power in existence that can disconnect me from the love of my Father.

I Am Chosen

God chose you before you were born. He's had a watchful eye on you since before you knew He even existed. God has specially handpicked you; you are God's elect. You are part of His royal priesthood, a brother or sister in His pursuit to bring hope to a world in despair. You have a purpose on this earth, and regardless of the mistakes you've made, where your current situation in life is, what responsibilities you have—no matter how insecure and weak you may feel— God still picks you!

He has big plans for your life, and He is the support you need to accomplish them. God gives you His joy, peace, wisdom, insight, confidence, and strength to accomplish your destiny and to help His people. He's given you all of your gifts, talents, and passions. You are chosen by the Creator of the universe; accept this affirmation and let it empower you to follow the passions and dreams He has placed inside you. The question is, will *you* choose *God*?

It is your choice whether you allow God to play a significant role in your life or not. Don't let insecurity and fear choke the life out of your dreams like it has with so many. Instead, put faith behind your passion and believe that against all odds you will be who God has called you to be. Be the man or woman you have always dreamed you could be! Face the opposition, face the potential embarrassment, and face the fear of the unknown head on with a fiery passion untamed and unhindered by small thinking and small living. God will not let down His chosen.

Scriptures

"But you are the ones chosen by God, chosen for the high calling of priestly work, chosen to be a holy people, God's instruments to do his work and speak out for him, to tell others of the night-and-day difference he made for you—from nothing to something, from rejected to accepted."

–1 Peter 2:9-10 (MSG)

"Even as [in His love] He chose us [actually picked us out for Himself as His own] in Christ before the foundation of the world, that we should be holy (consecrated and set apart for Him) and blameless in His sight, even above reproach, before Him in love."

–Ephesians 1:4 (AMPC)

"Furthermore, because we are united with Christ, we have received an inheritance from God, for he chose us in advance, and he makes everything work out according to his plan."

–Ephesians 1:11 (NLT)

Speak these words over your life

I am chosen by God; I am part of His chosen generation. I was handpicked by God. He has a plan and purpose for my life. I will fulfill the destiny God has for me. God has placed gifts and talents inside me to be used for His kingdom. I will not allow thoughts of my own inadequacies to rob me of the confidence that comes from being chosen of God. I know where I am weak, God is strong. God equips, empowers, and makes me ready for any task which He has set before me. I was chosen to come into this earth for such a time as this; I have a purpose that God has destined for me to fulfill. I will walk in confidence daily knowing just how much I matter in the eyes of the Lord.

I Am Righteous

You are the righteousness of Christ! This statement simply means that you are in right standing with God. When Christ died on the cross, He paid the cost for our sins—past, present, and future—and He replaced them with His own righteousness. Jesus came to this earth to make that trade so that we could have the same relationship and right standing with God that He did. Jesus gave us His ability to approach God any time of day, to talk to God as a friend, to call God Father, and to depend on God without shame—all in exchange for our sin. That's what it means to be the righteousness of Christ—God sees us like He does Jesus, because of Jesus. The Bible says Adam separated us from God by sin, but Jesus connects us to the Father through His righteousness.

When God sees you in pain and being tortured by shame, bound by guilt, and feeling as if you deserve to be punished and not forgiven, it hurts

Him. He gave everything so you wouldn't have to feel that way. He loves you, and He sees you spotless, just like Jesus. You are His child, and He wants you to be bold in His presence, not to act like you're a disgrace when you approach Him. Believe that the blood of Jesus Christ is more powerful than any sin you've committed—your past can't haunt you, your present is secure, and your future is bright. Believe you are the righteousness of Christ.

Scriptures

"For our sake He made Christ [virtually] to be sin Who knew no sin, so that in and through Him we might become [endued with, viewed as being in, and examples of] the righteousness of God [what we ought to be, approved and acceptable and in right relationship with Him, by His goodness]."

–2 CORINTHIANS 5:21 (AMPC)

"Namely, the righteousness of God which comes by believing with personal trust and confident reliance on Jesus Christ (the Messiah). [And it is meant] for all who believe. For there is no distinction,"

–ROMANS 3:22 (AMPC)

"If death ruled because of one person's failure, those who receive the multiplied grace and the gift of righteousness will even more certainly rule in life through the one person Jesus Christ."

–ROMANS 5:17 (CEB)

Speak these words over your life

The Bible says we have been made the righteousness of God, therefore in obedience to God's Word I boldly confess that I am the righteousness of God in Christ. Not by my goodness, not because I am holy within myself, but through the shed blood of Jesus, my Savior. His righteousness is His gift to me, and I will honor Christ's sacrifice by accepting it wholeheartedly. I have been made righteous and acceptable in the presence of my heavenly Father, and nothing that anyone says to me or about me can ever change that. I can go to God boldly when I need help and obtain grace and mercy. I am righteous not because of what I have done, but because of what Jesus has done for me.

I Am Loved

Whoever you are, whatever you have done, wherever you are from, no matter your station in life, God loves you and will never stop loving you. Neither your accomplishments nor your failures, your victories nor your defeats, qualify you or disqualify you for His love. Nothing you do or don't do will make God love you any more or any less. Let that truth set you free.

When God looks at you, He doesn't think paying with the most precious thing He had in all of eternity, Jesus Christ, was too high of a price for you. He displayed for all creation and eternity His immeasurable and untouchable love for you. That kind of love is difficult to comprehend, because it is so contrary to everything we see in this world. His love cannot be altered, changed, or stopped. It's unconditional. You can't earn it, you can't do enough good deeds to deserve it, and you can't do enough bad deeds for Him to take it away. But it is up to you whether you accept it or not.

When you sin, don't run from God—run *to* Him regardless of how big, bad, and ugly your sins have been, because God is not fazed by it. Nothing you can do is more powerful than what Jesus already did at the cross. Let Him break the bondage in your life, lift the weights off your shoulders, rid you of your guilt, heal your pain, take your worry, and replace your fear with faith born through an intimate relationship with Him. He wants to restore you with His love to a life of peace and joy. Rejoice, for you are loved!

Scriptures

"For I am convinced [and continue to be convinced—beyond any doubt] that neither death, nor life, nor angels, nor principalities, nor things present *and* threatening, nor things to come, nor powers, nor height, nor depth, nor any other created thing, will be able to separate us from the [unlimited] love of God, which is in Christ Jesus our Lord."

–Romans 8:38-39 (AMP)

"For God so loved the world, that he gave his only begotten Son, that whosoever believeth in him should not perish, but have everlasting life."

–John 3:16 (KJV)

"Love never fails [it never fades nor ends]….."

–1 Corinthians 13:8a (AMP)

"But because of his great love for us, God, who is rich in mercy, made us alive with Christ even when we were dead in transgressions—it is by grace you have been saved."

–Ephesians 2:4-5 (NIV)

Speak these words over your life

God's love for me is an unchangeable fact. God's love for me is greater than any sin I have committed, greater than any failure I have had. Nothing I do, nothing other people do, and nothing the devil does can separate me from God's love. Not death, nor life, nor angels or principalities can separate me from His love. God's love for me is eternal. His love knows no boundaries; it never gives up believing in me or reaching out to me. God's love is there for me in the darkest times in my life; when I think I can't go on. His love comforts me, His love sustains me, and His love encourages my soul and restores my hope. God's love endures forever, and He loves me.

I Am an Ambassador

The dictionary defines an ambassador as a diplomatic official of the highest rank who is sent by one sovereign nation to another as its resident representative. The Bible says plainly that we are Christ's ambassadors and God is making His appeal to a lost world through us. We are Christ's personal representatives! This means that you are a divine representative of Christ on this earth; you are an ambassador for Christ and the Kingdom of Heaven.

God touches the broken, brings healing to the hurting, restores relationships, instills peace, promotes joy, and affirms the insecure through you—His spokesperson and ambassador on this earth. As God's representatives, we have a duty and privilege to behave in such a manner that brings honor to God. We are not here on earth to fuse with it, and too often as Christians we try to blend in and exalt our problems in an attempt to relate to those around us. We end up hurt, broken, and confused like the people we are trying to help.

As ambassadors of Christ we are to walk in love like Jesus did, to live *in* the world but not *like* the world so we can help the world. For many people, we are the only God they will ever see, and we are the only Bible they will ever read. With this is mind, the attributes of Jesus should be evident in our lives. It's the joy and peace we have that people crave; it's the patience and gentleness that displays a love that people need; it's self-control and integrity that people respect and trust; and it's our generosity that separates us from a selfish society. That is the heart and soul of what it means to be an ambassador of Christ.

Scriptures

"So we are Christ's ambassadors, God making His appeal as it were through us. We [as Christ's personal representatives] beg you for His sake to lay hold of the divine favor [now offered you] and be reconciled to God."

–2 CORINTHIANS 5:20 (AMPC)

"But our citizenship is in heaven. And we eagerly await a Savior from there, the Lord Jesus Christ,"

–PHILIPPIANS 3:20 (NIV)

"And He called to Him the Twelve [apostles] and began to send them out [as His ambassadors] two by two and gave them authority and power over the unclean spirits."

–MARK 6:7 (AMPC)

"Therefore become imitators of God [copy Him and follow His example], as well-beloved children [imitate their father];"

–EPHESIANS 5:1 (AMPC)

Speak these words over your life

I am an ambassador of the Most High God and His Kingdom. I will represent my Father with honor, integrity, and dignity. I will live a life of purity and holiness before God. I am an ambassador of God's love, peace, and mercy to this world. I am quick to forgive the mistakes and shortcomings of others and myself. I am an ambassador of God's healing power, ready and available to be a blessing at all times and speak words of encouragement, hope, and healing to others. I am an ambassador of the power and might of the Holy Spirit and His anointing, and all it represents. I respond to adversity and calamity with a confident and peaceful spirit. I am resolute and undaunted in my faith. God provides His ability and His insight concerning my affairs. I will endeavor to conduct my life at all times in a manner that will be pleasing to Him.

I Am Redeemed

Adam's disobedience opened the door for sin and death to enter the world, separating people from God. Seeing His children suffering due to the effects of sin, God sent Jesus to pay the price of sin and redeem mankind. To redeem something is to gain or regain possession of it in exchange for payment. When you say you are redeemed, you are declaring that **God bought you back!**

This world is in a state of decay from all the effects of sin. Sickness, disease, poverty, pestilence, lack, every kind of hurt, and everything that is diabolical has come upon the earth. Deuteronomy 28 lists every sort of terrible affliction that people face as the result of their disobedience and sin. This list is known as the Curse of the Law. It clearly says that everything that is bad is of the curse. But though the curse may wreak havoc *all around* you, it has no power *over* you because you are redeemed!

You were destined for a life of pain leading to death. But because this misery that was to be our lives was unbearable to God, despite all that you have done to deserve judgment, He bought you back. He ripped you out of the clutches of a doomed existence and accepted you as part of His family. You are redeemed out of the curse and into His blessings. His redemption covers you for the here and now, past, present, and future. You are God's child, bought by the blood of Christ. You are God's once again, for you are redeemed.

Scriptures

"In him we have redemption through his blood, the forgiveness of sins, in accordance with the riches of God's grace that he lavished on us. With all wisdom and understanding,"

–EPHESIANS 1:7-8 (NIV)

"Who gave himself for us to redeem us from all wickedness and to purify for himself a people that are his very own, eager to do what is good."

–TITUS 2:14 (NIV)

"Christ purchased our freedom and redeemed us from the curse of the Law and its condemnation by becoming a curse for us"

–GALATIANS 3:13 A (AMP)

"But it is from Him that you are in Christ Jesus, who became to us wisdom from God [revealing His plan of salvation], and righteousness [making us acceptable to God], and sanctification [making us holy and setting us apart for God], and redemption [providing our ransom from the penalty for sin],"

–1 CORINTHIANS 1:30 (AMP)

Speak these words over your life

I am redeemed. My spirit is full of life and united with God. I am redeemed from any and all failures. I am redeemed from any and all addictions. I am redeemed from the curse of the law. I am redeemed from sin, sickness, and an eternity spent apart from God. Because of the price Jesus paid for my redemption, I can and will declare with boldness:

I am free; I am strong; I am a light in the darkness. I am an overcomer; I am a child of the Almighty. I am chosen; I am righteous; I am loved. I am an ambassador; I am favored; I am protected. I am more than a conqueror; I am healed; I am prosperous. I am the temple of the Holy Spirit; I am rooted in Christ; I am complete.

I Am Complete

It's easy to look in the mirror and notice every flaw about you. If you want to feel bad about yourself, then compare your looks to the top models, your intelligence to the top minds, and your relationship with God to the great leaders of faith.

Yet while you might not be able to compare when you focus on the brilliant minds, the most attractive people, and the most devout believers, if you will shift your focus to Christ, the creator of the universe, you will find they don't even come close to His perfection! Stop comparing the "Goliath" in your life with the "shepherd boy" David you see in the mirror; instead do what David did and compare your greatest obstacle to *God*. Because when you compare anything to God, no matter how big it is, God is bigger still!

You are complete in Christ. Where you are weak, He is strong. Where you have failed a thousand times, with Him you will overcome. When you are sick, He makes you whole. When your heart is broken, His love knits it back together. When you have no more fight left, He's your endurance that picks you up and carries you across the finish line. Forgiver of sins, emotional and physical Healer, constant Companion through every trial, Protector from all danger, He is everything you need. You've been made a child of the Almighty, freed from everything holding you back, and have a promise of a bright future. All this is given to you through the death and resurrection of Christ so that you can be complete! Believe it—no matter what insecurities you battle, what obstacle is in front of you, how inadequate you feel, or how big your mistakes are—with God you are ready and equal to anything. You are complete in Christ.

Scriptures

"And in Him you have been made complete [achieving spiritual stature through Christ], and He is the head over all rule and authority [of every angelic and earthly power]."

–Colossians 2:10 (AMP)

"All Scripture is breathed out by God and profitable for teaching, for reproof, for correction, and for training in righteousness, that the man of God may be complete, equipped for every good work."

–2 Timothy 3:16-17 (ESV)

"But He has said to me, 'My grace is sufficient for you [My lovingkindness and My mercy are more than enough—always available—regardless of the situation]; for [My] power is being perfected [and is completed and shows itself most effectively] in [your] weakness.' Therefore, I will all the more gladly boast in my weaknesses, so that the power of Christ [may completely enfold me and] may dwell in me."

–2 Corinthians 12:9 (AMP)

Speak these words over your life

My salvation is a gift from God. There is nothing I did to earn it. There is nothing I can do to improve on it. I was broken and empty before I met Jesus, but when I accepted Jesus as my personal Savior, He came into me, filling all the gaps of my inadequacies, imperfections, and flaws. He filled my emptiness with His Love; my loneliness with His friendship; my weakness with His strength; my failures with His forgiveness; my worries with His peace; my stress with His joy; my sickness with His healing; my inability with His ability; my insecurity with His confidence; my fears with faith. Any area in which I come up short when it comes to my own ability, God makes up the difference with His ability. I am complete because Christ is in me and He is with me.

I Am Protected

The world is a dangerous place; violent crime is on the rise, terrorism has become a global menace, and sickness continues to plague our society. But we don't need to subscribe to the daily dose of fear the world prescribes, for God refers to Himself as a shield, a refuge, a strong tower, and a very present help in trouble.

The Lord protects us through the power of His Word and by the leading of His Holy Spirit. When you confess His divine protection over your life, you are releasing the power in His words to halt any force that would seek to harm you, and you are increasing your sensitivity to His warnings of danger. God will protect you by warning you to stay away from harmful situations. Listen to these warnings, for they are your answer to prayer and the result of your confession. His protection extends past the physical dangers in the world; He'll also protect you emotionally as well. He'll warn you against harmful relationships, and He'll even guard your heart so that though you hear harsh words, they don't seem to affect you like they used to.

God takes it seriously when you call Him your shield. He cannot and will not allow His child, who is confessing His promises back to Him, to be harmed. He looks throughout the entire world to show Himself strong on behalf of men and women like that. Designate a few moments in the morning to the declaration of His protection over you and your family, and walk the rest of the day free from the fear of this world's ability to harm you.

Scriptures

"My God is my rock, in whom I find protection. He is my shield, the power that saves me, and my place of safety. He is my refuge, my savior, the one who saves me from violence. I called on the Lord, who is worthy of praise, and he saved me from my enemies."

–2 Samuel 22:3-4 (NLT)

"God is our refuge and strength [mighty and impenetrable], a very present *and* well-proved help in trouble."

–Psalm 46:1 (AMP)

"A thousand may fall at your side, ten thousand at your right hand, but it will not come near you."

–Psalm 91:7 (NIV)

"In peace I will lie down and sleep, for you alone, O Lord, will keep me safe."

–Psalm 4:8 (NLT)

Speak these words over your life

Wherever I go and whatever I do, I am walking under the covering of God's divine protection. The angels of the Lord go with me and before me to protect me and keep me from all harm, danger, and calamity. I am attentive to hear God's warnings. The Lord is my refuge and my strength; my fortress and strong tower. I will not fear, for the Lord is with me. I will not fear any evil for I am protected by the Lord! I am protected from financial scams, from violent crimes, from automobile accidents, from adverse weather, and from injuries while at work or at the gym. No evil shall befall me; no plague shall come near my household. My home, my family, and all those who are in my company are protected by God Almighty.

I Am More Than a Conqueror

It is not God's will for you to be defeated, discouraged, or depressed. In fact, it is just the opposite. The Bible clearly tells us that through Christ Jesus we are more than conquerors. That means regardless of what challenges come your way, no matter what life tries to do to bring you down, in spite of the impossible situation you might find yourself in—with God's help you can conquer it. God's will for you is total victory in every area of your life!

Whatever has been holding you back, you can conquer it. Maybe it's bad habits, financial pressure, or a health condition. God is your redeemer, your provider, and your healer. You will conquer it with Him as your ally. Even if you are being held back by internal struggles, such as regret, fear, anxiety, or depression, God sent His Spirit to revitalize, renew, and empower you from the inside out.

You may feel as though you are in a pit of despair that is so deep you could never get out. But God is the God of hope, and He will rescue you. Nothing you are facing is bigger than your God. Whatever the struggle, whether it's external or internal, God is in you and God is for you. You can count on Him to be with you, facing down any obstacle. You can face your problems head on and defeat them. It's time to rise up; it's time to stand strong. You have the Spirit of a conqueror inside you, so awaken the dormant, unstoppable power within your spirit. Begin to speak God's promises over your life. You are more than a conqueror.

Scriptures

"Nay, in all these things we are more than conquerors through him that loved us."

–ROMANS 8:37 (KJV)

"But if the Spirit of him that raised up Jesus from the dead dwell in you, he that raised up Christ from the dead shall also quicken your mortal bodies by his Spirit that dwelleth in you."

–ROMANS 8:11 (KJV)

"But thanks be to God, Who gives us the victory [making us conquerors] through our Lord Jesus Christ."

–1 CORINTHIANS 15:57 (AMPC)

"Who is it that is victorious over [that conquers] the world but he who believes that Jesus is the Son of God [who adheres to, trusts in, and relies on that fact]?"

–1 JOHN 5:5 (AMPC)

Speak these words over your life

I am more than a conqueror through Christ; I am ready for anything and equal to anything. The same Spirit that raised Christ from the dead dwells within me. Just as Jesus conquered the grave, I shall conquer any challenge that dares to confront me today. I have the Spirit of victory in me. With God's help, I can and will conquer my problems. I am self-sufficient in Christ's sufficiency. I am well able to endure, battle, and conquer with God as my ally, and my faith in Him as my shield. There is nothing that I face today that can stop me from my relentless trust in my God. I am convinced that God is faithful. He is on my side; He is for me; He is with me; and He is in me. So I stand undaunted, full of vigor, ready for life, knowing that nothing can stand against me when I'm united with God.

I Am Prosperous

God takes pleasure in blessing you, and it's His will for you to be prosperous. God does not want you in lack for any reason, and He wants you to thrive in life, always having more than enough!

One of the names of God in the Bible is *El Shaddai,* which translates into "the God that is more than enough." God is a "too much" God! He doesn't deal in just enough—He deals in abundance. It's His plan for your life to have enough to take care of all your needs and be a blessing to others, too! To be able to take your family out for a nice meal, to live in a good home, to drive a great car, to go on a nice vacation, and to be able to bless others as you have been blessed.

Sometimes it can be daunting to think that you could live this abundant life, but don't be discouraged about your situation, just start where you are. Believe God for a little extra to give, and a little extra to enjoy, and speak His promises of abundance over your life. As time passes, your faith will increase as well as your ability to receive abundance in your finances. Your words have power to shape your life when filled with faith in God. Declare that He supplies all of your needs according to His riches in glory, expect His prosperity in your life, and thank Him before you see any change because you know it's coming! Do this and watch God show Himself strong on your behalf. You are the child of El Shaddai—you are prosperous.

Scriptures

"And God is able to make all grace (every favor and earthly blessing) come to you in abundance, so that you may always *and* under all circumstances *and* whatever the need be self-sufficient [possessing enough to require no aid or support and furnished in abundance for every good work and charitable donation]."

–2 Corinthians 9:8 (AMPC)

"But my God shall supply all your need according to his riches in glory by Christ Jesus."

–Philippians 4:19 (KJV)

"Now to Him Who, by (in consequence of) the [action of His] power that is at work within us, is able to [carry out His purpose and] do superabundantly, far over *and* above all that we [dare] ask or think [infinitely beyond our highest prayers, desires, thoughts, hopes, or dreams]."

–Ephesians 3:20 (AMPC)

"Let the Lord be magnified, which hath pleasure in the prosperity of his servant."

–Psalm 35:27 (b) (KJV)

Speak these words over your life

I am abundantly blessed. God takes care of me. I will not worry or be anxious about my finances, because my God shall supply all of my needs according to His riches in Glory. I always, under all circumstances, have whatever I need. I am sufficient in Christ, for it is He who is able to do far more abundantly than all I can ask or think. God gives me wisdom, insight, and favor concerning all my financial affairs. I am successful; I am prosperous; I declare I have more than enough money to take care of all my needs and plenty left over to be a generous giver towards others and the Kingdom of God. God takes pleasure in my prosperity. I will walk in prosperity all the days of my life, and I will give honor and glory to my God with the abundance He has given me.

I Am the Temple of the Holy Spirit

The Bible calls you the temple of the Holy Spirit. The Bible also says that the same Spirit that raised Jesus Christ from the dead now lives in you! The Holy Spirit is in you to comfort you when you are feeling down. He's in you to remind you who you are in Christ when your actions dictate something else entirely. He's in you to guide you through life so that you will be full of joy and perfect peace as you walk towards the purpose that God has destined for you. He's in you to equip you with the knowledge and wisdom you need as problems arise. He's in you to give you energy when you run out of steam. He's in you to unveil the truth and splendor of God's character as you study His Word to grow in understanding. He's in you to infuse life, light, and love into the hurting and dying world—through you!

Being a temple of the Holy Spirit means you house this magnificent blessing within yourself. Living this means you rely on God's direction through the leading of His Spirit. Understanding this tells you that you are not in this fight alone, but rather you have the Spirit of the Lord within you to fight with you and for you.

He is the ultimate help in your time of need. He's your constant companion, your support, and your comforter. He's your friend, and when you need His help He'll show up every time, for it's the very Spirit of your Heavenly Father that lives in you. If you have never let the Holy Spirit play a role in your life, then you are in for a blessed adventure when you accept that you are the temple of the Holy Spirit.

Scriptures

"Do you not know that your bodies are temples of the Holy Spirit, who is in you, whom you have received from God? You are not your own;"

–1 Corinthians 6:19 (NIV)

"Don't you know that you yourselves are God's temple and that God's Spirit dwells in your midst?"

–1 Corinthians 3:16 (NIV)

"If the Spirit of him who raised Jesus from the dead dwells in you, he who raised Christ Jesus from the dead will also give life to your mortal bodies through his Spirit who dwells in you."

–Romans 8:11 (ESV)

"But the Comforter (Counselor, Helper, Intercessor, Advocate, Strengthener, Standby), the Holy Spirit, Whom the Father will send in My name [in My place, to represent Me and act on My behalf], He will teach you all things. And He will cause you to recall (will remind you of, bring to your remembrance) everything I have told you."

–John 14:26 (AMPC)

Speak these words over your life

My body is the temple of the Holy Spirit. God's Spirit lives in me. I am not my own; I belong to Him. I am the temple of the living God. God dwells in me, and works in me and through me. He is my God and I am His child. I choose to treat my body in a way that will honor God. The Holy Spirit in me gives me courage, strength, and power to fulfill God's plan for my life. He gives me wisdom and insight concerning all the affairs of my life. He is my comforter, my encourager, my best friend, my mentor, and my protector. He reveals the truths of His Word and makes them real to me. I am keen to hear and quick to obey the direction and counsel of the Holy Spirit.

I Am Rooted

Victorious strength, unyielding faith, and reckless tenacity come through the Spirit of faith living in every Word of God. Being rooted in Christ is planting your life within the solid ground of His infallible Word and digging your roots deep in Him so you can utilize every gift that has been given to empower and revitalize you.

You are like a tree—the deeper your roots grow, the stronger you are. Not only do a tree's roots draw nutrients from the soil to feed the entire body, but they also act as an anchor when the storm winds blow against it. It's the roots that keep a tree firmly planted! When a crisis roars into your life like a raging storm, it's time to stand on the promises in God's Word. When you are in a drought, the stressful grind of life doesn't seem to end, and your strength is all but faded, you draw the energy from deep within where the streams of living water flow, for when you are weak God is strong. You are rooted in Christ.

His Word is your foundation, but how deep your roots go into that foundation is up to you. The more you read His Word, the more you spend time thinking about it, the more you speak it, the more aware of His things you become, and the more fulfilling your relationship with God becomes, the deeper your roots will go. Identify with the Word of God, draw from it, and let it reshape your mind, repurpose your direction, and rejuvenate your body. The Bible is God speaking to you, so be firmly rooted in God's unshakable Word!

Scripture:

"Then Christ will make his home in your hearts as you trust in him. Your roots will grow down into God's love and keep you strong. And may you have the power to understand, as all God's people should, how wide, how long, how high, and how deep his love is."

–Ephesians 3:17-18 (NLT)

"Blessed [with spiritual security] is the man who believes *and* trusts in *and* relies on the Lord and whose hope *and* confident expectation is the Lord. For he will be [nourished] like a tree planted by the waters, that spreads out its roots by the river; and will not fear the heat when it comes; but its leaves will be green *and* moist. And it will not be anxious *and* concerned in a year of drought nor stop bearing fruit."

–Jeremiah 17:7-8 (AMP)

Speak these words over your life

I am rooted deeply in the Word of God. The Word of God is my foundation. It is my source of strength, confidence, hope, and faith. My life is secure because its foundation is the unchangeable and unshakable truth that is the Word of God. The Word of God will keep me anchored when the storms of life come. Because I am rooted in Christ, I will remain strong, stable, and unafraid in the middle of even the scariest circumstance. When faced with difficulties and challenges I don't know how to handle, I will not fret or be dismayed. I will remain resolute, with my eyes fixed on Christ, and my faith rooted deep in His Word. I shall not be moved. His Word gives me courage and fortitude to endure, preserve, and overcome whatever comes my way.

I HAVE

WHAT THE BIBLE SAYS I HAVE

Introduction

Many Christians walk through life woefully unaware of the arsenal of God's gifts that they have at their disposal. The Bible tells us that when we accept Jesus as our Savior, we are adopted into God's family. God becomes our Father, and as His children we gain access to all our loving Father has to offer.

God is not ignorant of the pressures, problems, and temptations that we all face. That is why God has given you His support and the equipment you need to rise above every issue that arises in your life. All of His gifts are already yours! You don't have to sacrifice anything to obtain them, you don't have to live a perfect life to earn them, and you don't have to work really hard to be worthy of them. All you have to do is accept them just as you are.

God gave us life so that He could have children to love and spend time with. He has given us a purpose to accomplish so that we know that we are important and unique to Him. He gave us hope so that no matter how tragic life seems, we can know He is by our side and will help us get through any crisis. He gave us grace so that nothing could come between Him and His kids. He placed Jesus at His right hand, giving Him the position as our Advocate so that Jesus can relay our heart to the Father with perfect accuracy.

God gave us His protection so that we can walk confidently in obedience with him without fear. He gave us supernatural peace that passes all human understanding so we can navigate the tumultuous waters of this life with confidence and a triumphant spirit. He gave us authority and dominion to walk as His ambassadors on this earth. He has given us His provision so we will have all that we need—and plenty more to achieve our destiny and bless multitudes of people along the way. He gave us the promise of healing so that we would not live in hurt and pain or be stopped from accomplishing our mission on this earth. He gave us wisdom for all of life's decisions. He gave us faith and victory to overcome any trial, and He gave us a way out so that we are never at the mercy of our circumstances.

Jesus' sacrifice bought us back from destruction, and now we have a position of prominence with the Father. God gave us a position in His kingdom, a way of living on this earth as our inheritance just because we belong to him. He gave us His Spirit, to reside in us and to convey the truths of His Word and His love to us. He is our Guide, Mentor, and Counselor, and He empowers us with the same resurrection power that raised Christ Jesus from the dead so that we can triumph over any situation with the spirit of a conqueror.

And this is only scratching the surface. God's gifts are waiting for you! All you need to do is to reach out and grab them and operate in His divine strength, peace, and joy.

Chapter 1

I Have a Father

When you accepted Jesus as your personal Savior, the Bible says that you become part of God's family, a child of God. God became your Father!

Jesus' main purpose in coming to the earth was to connect God's kids back with Him—not just a superficial relationship but a close and intimate connection with your Father. We tend to overcomplicate what it means to be a Christian, but when you boil the Christian message down you get a very simple truth:

We were created in the likeness of God *because God wanted children,* and when humanity messed up, He valued us so much that He sent Jesus to die to buy His children back.

When Jesus was on earth, He referred to God as "Abba," which translates in our modern language to "Daddy." It's an intimate name for father that we can now call Him. When you need help with a problem or you simply need a friend, you have your Daddy to talk to.

He cares for you, loves you, and wants a close relationship with you. He wants to spend time with you, to walk through life with you, to laugh with you, and to be a shoulder for you to cry on. He wants to protect you from any danger. He wants to give you Fatherly advice and help you make the right decision. He wants you to be happy, at peace, and flourishing in whatever you do.

He knows the number of hairs on your head, He knit you together in the womb, and He knew you and loved you even before you breathed your first breath. He is your Daddy—there is no mistake He can't forgive, there is no sickness He can't heal, and there is no situation that He can't solve. He gave you His Spirit, and a guidebook we call the Bible, to help you navigate through the tumultuous waters of everyday life. So, run to your Father with your problems, with your mistakes, and with all your insecurities, because He loves you unconditionally and wants you to enjoy your life as His child.

Scriptures

But for us, There is one God, the Father, by whom all things were created, and for whom we live. And there is one Lord, Jesus Christ, through whom all things were created, and through whom we live.

–1 CORINTHIANS 8:6 (NLT)

See what kind of love the Father has given to us, that we should be called children of God; and so we are. The reason why the world does not know us is that it did not know him.

–1 JOHN 3:1 (ESV)

And you did not receive the "spirit of religious duty," leading you back into the fear *of never being good enough.* But you have received the "Spirit of full acceptance," enfolding you into the family of God. And you will never feel orphaned, for as he rises up within us, our spirits join him in saying the words of tender affection, "Beloved Father!"

–ROMANS 8:15 (TPT)

Speak These Words Over Your Life

I am a child of God, God is my heavenly Father. I have a solid connection, an untouchable bond, and a relationship that cannot diminish with Him. My Father loves me unconditionally, and there is nothing that can separate me from His love. It knows no bounds. He forgives me of all my sins. His love and grace fill my heart with fullness of joy. He loves me in spite of my short-coming and inadequacies. My reliance on my Father God gets me through the day, causes me to overcome every adverse circumstance that I face, and gives me the confidence, courage, and ability to achieve greatness. It is my reliance on my Father God that sets me apart and gives me exactly what I need to accomplish every task that I am assigned. My Father has displayed His love for me in a way that will cause me never to doubt His willingness or His ability to come through for me. So, I boldly declare that My God is my Father and I will live my life for Him.

Chapter 2

I Have a Purpose and a Destiny

We all have had hopes and dreams of accomplishing something significant in our lives, but as we grow older those dreams and desires are shoved to the back of our minds as the responsibilities, obligations, and the demands of life begin to take their place.

You may feel as though you have wasted too much time and let your opportunity pass you by. You may feel that greatness is simply not in the cards for you anymore, but there is good news for you. God has a history of using imperfect people to accomplish great things. So regardless of time wasted or sins committed, regardless of your numerous responsibilities or obligations, regardless of any insecurities or hopelessness you may experience, GOD STILL PICKS YOU.

You have a purpose; you have a destiny. There is a task that no one else can accomplish the way God meant it to be accomplished except you.

There is a place that you will flourish. There is a future of fulfillment and contentment ahead of you. You don't have to know how—or even what—all you have to do is open up your heart and be willing to follow God's plan and destiny for your life.

Many worry about what their destiny and purpose is exactly. They want to please God but have no idea where to start. The Bible says when you seek after God, you will find Him, and when you draw near to God, He will draw near to you. When you draw close to God and seek His will, a beautiful moment occurs as the weight in your life melts away as He teaches you how to live freely and lightly. God will reveal His plan and destiny for your life as you honor Him with your time, read His words, speak His words over your life, worship Him, and by praying to Him, laying your whole heart before Him. With your eyes fixed on God chasing after Him with all your heart, you'll find yourself right in the middle of your destiny.

Scriptures

"For I know the plans I have for you," declares the Lord, "plans to prosper you and not to harm you, plans to give you hope and a future."

–Jeremiah 29:11 (NIV)

"I pray with great faith for you, because I'm fully convinced that the One who began this glorious work in you will faithfully continue the process of maturing you and will put his finishing touches to it until the unveiling of our Lord Jesus Christ!"

–Philippians 1:6 (TPT)

"For those whom He foreknew and loved and chose beforehand, He also predestined to be conformed to the image of His Son and ultimately share in His complete sanctification, so that He would be the firstborn the most beloved and honored among many believers. And those whom He predestined, He also called; and those whom He called, He also justified declared free of the guilt of sin; and those whom He justified, He also glorified raising them to a heavenly dignity."

–Romans 8:29-30 (AMP)

Speak These Words Over Your Life

I shall fulfill my God-given destiny. Regardless of what excuses or obstacles I have allowed to hold me back in the past, I choose, right now, to cast aside every weight and every hindrance and to wholeheartedly pursue the plans and purposes God has for my life. He has given me purpose in life and called me into a grand destiny; I will not doubt my purpose. My God shall provide the necessary resources, the favor, and the opportunities to fulfill all He has destined for my life. I will not give up on the dreams God has given me. I will keep my eyes fixed on Him and accomplish all the plans that God has for me.

Chapter 3

I Have a Hope

Contrary to what most people believe, when the Bible refers to the word "hope," it is not referring to wishful thinking. Biblical hope is a spiritual force—confident trust in God, believing without reservation that God is on your side and will see you through any situation. Hope is the foundation for faith. Hope is the expectation of a better tomorrow because you know God is with you and is willing and able to help you, sustain you, and provide a path to victory for you.

You may not have any idea how or when your life is going to improve, how or when your dreams are going to be accomplished, how or when your storm will cease, but hope knows that it will because God is faithful and He will not let His child fail.

God loves you so deeply that He made a promise to you—no matter how cruel life seems, He will be there by your side to be your Friend, to help you, to strengthen you, and to provide a way out. He is our hope, He is our future, and He is our guarantee. You can have faith in His love for you, His ability to help you, and His willingness to make a way on your behalf.

Even if you find yourself in a tough spot, whether it's a huge problem or a minor issue, God will turn even the worst situations around for you. He'll shelter you in the storms of life—not just to escape them and hide, but to gain strength and renew your hope. Hope will sustain you in the middle of life's greatest difficulties. God will give you patience to endure, strength to persevere, and courage to overcome whatever challenges you may be facing. He'll make a way when there seems to be no way out. So smile and let your heart overflow with hope because what's impossible with man is possible with God!

Scriptures

For whatever was written in earlier times was written for our instruction, so that through endurance and the encouragement of the Scriptures we might have hope *and* overflow with confidence in His promises.

–ROMANS 15:4 (AMP)

So it is impossible for God to lie for we know that his promise and his vow will never change! And now we have run into his heart to hide ourselves in his faithfulness. This is where we find his strength and comfort, for he empowers us to seize what has already been established ahead of time—an unshakeable hope! We have this certain hope like a strong, unbreakable anchor holding our souls to God himself. Our anchor of hope is fastened *to the mercy seat* which sits in the heavenly realm beyond the sacred threshold.

–HEBREWS 6:18-19 (TPT)

Now may God, the inspiration and fountain of hope, fill you to overflowing with uncontainable joy and perfect peace as you trust in him. And may the power of the Holy Spirit continually surround your life with his super-abundance until you radiate with hope!

–ROMANS 15:13 (TPT)

Speak These Words Over Your Life

My Hope is in God—not in myself, others, or in this world's system. He is my refuge, and He is my strength. He is my deliverer. He will never leave me or forsake me. He will sustain me and lift me up in troubled times. He is my hope. He encourages me, comforts me, and gives me peace through His Word and by the Holy Spirit. In the midst of adversity and difficulties, He gives me strength and courage to persevere. He loves me unconditionally, and He will never leave me to face the circumstances of life alone. In His promises, I find joy, peace, and hope.

Chapter 4

I Have Grace

Grace is a truly remarkable force. It is the action of, the all-inclusive demonstration of, and the immensely powerful representation of God's love for you.

God forgives you, loves you, and wants the best for you. His grace is how He displays that great love for you in your life. He sent Jesus to die on the cross so that He could give us grace! Its very purpose is to reunite you with your Father and to keep you there, free from the pressures of living a perfect life through your own acts of devotion and sacrifice.

God has put in your heart passions, desires, and dreams that He knew you could not accomplish on your own. Your high calling is to accomplish your dreams **with** Him. His grace is a source of strength for and a protector of that calling. It gives you influence with people, it provides opportunities for you, it eradicates anything that would try to disrupt and disconnect you from God, and if you do make a mistake and sin, then grace is also there to wipe your slate clean. There is nothing you have done or ever could do, there is not a sin in existence, that is more powerful than His grace. God doesn't want you living a life constantly aware of where you are falling short; He wants you to live a life fully aware of His love for you. Nobody is perfect, but God knew that so His grace makes up for all our imperfections and shortcomings.

Grace stands in the gap between the "you" that you want to be, and the "you" that you actually are through Jesus.

And His grace doesn't stop there! It digs deeper into your life, mending broken hearts, putting relationships back together, healing emotional scarring, and freeing you up from the weights you once carried! The best part about this wonderful display of God's affection is this simple truth: it's unmerited. If there were a way to earn it, then there would be a way to lose it. But God gives it to us freely, so take ahold and praise the Lord for His grace!

Scriptures

For it is by grace [God's remarkable compassion and favor drawing you to Christ] that you have been saved [actually delivered from judgment and given eternal life] through faith. And this [salvation] is not of yourselves [not through your own effort], but it is the [undeserved, gracious] gift of God; not as a result of [your] works [nor your attempts to keep the Law], so that no one will [be able to] boast or take credit in any way [for his salvation].

–EPHESIANS 2:8-9 (AMP)

But by the grace of God I am what I am, and his grace toward me was not in vain. On the contrary, I worked harder than any of them, though it was not I, but the grace of God that is with me.

–1 CORINTHIANS 15:10 (ESV)

And God is able to make all grace [every favor and earthly blessing] come in abundance to you, so that you may always [under all circumstances, regardless of the need] have complete sufficiency in everything [being completely self-sufficient in Him], and have an abundance for every good work and act of charity.

–2 CORINTHIANS 9:8 (AMP)

Speak These Words Over Your Life

I am thankful for the gift of God's grace in my life. I am immersed in His loving embrace through the display of His grace. His grace picks me up when I fall short, and it gives me hope to face tomorrow with confidence and courage. His grace is a constant reminder that God loves me unconditionally, and His forgiveness knows no bounds. His grace sustains me in times of adversity and difficulty. His grace encourages and strengthens me when faced with challenges in life. His grace inspires me and gives me hope.

His grace has put a smile on my face, peace in my mind, joy in my heart, and has given me the strength to accomplish my destiny on this earth.

Chapter 5

I Have an Advocate

The Bible tells us that when Jesus went back to heaven, He took His place at the right hand of God. He now lives to make intercession for us. Jesus is praying for you right now! How cool is that! He has become your Advocate.

An advocate is "a person who publicly supports or recommends a particular cause or policy, or a person who pleads on someone else's behalf." Your Advocate is revealed in 1 John 2:1:

"My dear children, I am writing this to you so that you will not sin. But if anyone does sin, we have an advocate who pleads our case before the Father. He is Jesus Christ, the one who is truly righteous" (NLT).

This is the very reason why when you pray to God, you end your prayer with, "in Jesus' name, amen." Your prayers don't have to be perfect because Jesus is, and when He hears what you're saying, He takes your heart and pleads your case to God for you. It's a sweet transition because Jesus knows precisely what you are going through. The Bible even says,

"For we do not have a High Priest who is unable to sympathize and understand our weaknesses and temptations, but One who has been tempted [knowing exactly how it feels to be human] in every respect as we are, yet without [committing any] sin." –Hebrews 4:15 (AMP)

That means He knows exactly what you are feeling and wants to help you with it. Before many of the miracles Jesus performed, the Bible notes that He had compassion on them. Jesus loves you and feels the pain you've been going through. So when you feel inadequate, like you have let God down too many times, you don't have enough faith, and you are wondering why your prayers would be answered because you don't know the right words to say, remember that you can pour out your heart before God. Jesus will fill in the gaps of all your inadequacies and lack of faith, and He reminds God of His Word. Praise the Lord for Jesus, our Advocate!

Scriptures

For there is one God, and one mediator between God and men, the man Christ Jesus.

–1 Timothy 2:5 (KJV)

For Christ has entered, not into holy places made with hands, which are copies of the true things, but into heaven itself, now to appear in the presence of God on our behalf.

–Hebrews 9:24 (ESV)

Just think how much more the blood of Christ will purify our consciences from sinful deeds so that we can worship the living God. For by the power of the eternal Spirit, Christ offered himself to God as a perfect sacrifice for our sins. That is why he is the one who mediates a new covenant between God and people, so that all who are called can receive the eternal inheritance God has promised them. For Christ died to set them free from the penalty of the sins they had committed under that first covenant.

–Hebrews 9:14-15 (NLT)

Speak These Words Over Your Life

Jesus is my Lord, my Savior, and my Advocate. He has taken His seat of authority at the right hand of God. He now lives to make intercession for me. He pleads my case before Father God. When I sin and fall short, it is through His blood that I am forgiven and made righteous. He was my substitute on the cross. He took my sins, shortcomings, and failures. It's not by works or anything that I have done, but by His blood, I have salvation and access to God's unconditional love. Jesus is my Advocate. He is my righteousness, He is my saving grace, and He is my friend! Praise the Lord for my Advocate!

Chapter 6

I Have an Inheritance

Congratulations! You have an inheritance. The Bible tells us that we are joint heirs with Jesus, children of the Most High God, and positioned to carry out His will on the earth as the heirs to His kingdom. With that title, you have been given an inheritance. No matter what your station in life or how unworthy you might feel, you have an inheritance. Not because you deserve it or have done anything to earn it—it is there because of what Jesus did *for you* out of God's great love for you.

Normally we equate inheritance to a sum of money that is left for us, and though the definition definitely encompasses money, it is not limited to the financial arena. Read these various ways "inherit" is defined, "receive (money, property, or a title) as an heir at the death of the previous holder." Another is, "derive (a quality, characteristic, or predisposition) genetically from one's parents or ancestors." And lastly, "receive or be left with (a situation, object, etc.) from a predecessor or former owner."

When God adopted you into His family, He gave you an inheritance. He gave you a title: "Child of God." He gave you His spirit to develop your character and disposition and to help cultivate a quality of life that you would truly enjoy. He gave you a situation in which you have access to your Father God at all times.

The Bible is full of promises and gifts just like these, that belong to you, His child. The Bible is God's personal letter to you; it is part of your inheritance. So read, discover, and enjoy what God has spoken to you and choose to accept the gifts He gave to you. Choose to accept the title, the quality of life, and the situation He gave you. Choose to accept the promise of abundant provision for every area of your life. Choose to accept strength for the storms of life. Choose to accept the peace that passes all understanding. Choose to accept deliverance from adversity. And the greatest of all, choose to accept salvation and eternal life—the ability to spend eternity with our Savior and Father God in heaven. Enjoy your inheritance!

Scriptures

In Him we also were made God's heritage (portion) *and* we obtained an inheritance; for we had been foreordained (chosen and appointed beforehand) in accordance with His purpose, Who works out everything in agreement with the counsel *and* design of His own will.

–EPHESIANS 1:11 (AMPC)

Knowing [with all certainty] that it is from the Lord [and not from men] that you will receive the inheritance which is your [real] reward. [The One Whom] you are actually serving [is] the Lord Christ (the Messiah).

–COLOSSIANS 3:24 (AMPC)

Celebrate with praises the God and Father of our Lord Jesus Christ, who has shown us his extravagant mercy. For his *fountain of* mercy has given us a new life—we are reborn to experience a living, energetic hope through the resurrection of Jesus Christ from the dead. We are reborn into a perfect inheritance that can never perish, never be defiled, and never diminish. It is promised and preserved forever in the heavenly realm for you!

–1 PETER 1:3-4 (TPT)

Speak These Words Over Your Life

I have an inheritance. I am an heir of Christ, and as His heir, I receive what He has left me. All the promises that His Word contains belongs to me. My inheritance includes eternal life and a personal relationship with Jesus. I receive my provision, health, and the wisdom He has given to me, and therefore I declare that I am healthy, wealthy, and wise. I receive His peace that passes understanding, the joy that will strengthen me, and the love that will remind me who I am and what I mean to Him. I declare I am peaceful, joyful, and loved. I inherited the title of "child of the living God," so I refuse to degrade myself by thinking wrong thoughts, behaving in an inappropriate manner, and letting any foul things come out of my mouth. My inheritance in God is untouchable by the enemy, it cannot decay, and it cannot change or lessen in its life-changing potency.

Chapter 7

I Have the Greater One

When you accepted Jesus as your personal Savior, Jesus said His Spirit came to live in you. Jesus said He would make His home in you, and He even refers to our body as a temple to house His Spirit, the Holy Spirit of God Himself. This is the *same* Spirit that empowered Jesus on this earth to walk in God's divine will and the same Spirit that raised Jesus from the dead! That same Spirit now lives in *you*. He is there to guide, comfort, encourage, and ultimately empower you to do God's will upon the earth.

Greater is He that is in you than he *(Satan and the powers of darkness)* that is in the World.

He's greater than any storm that could come. He's greater than any crisis you could face. He's greater than any power that could come against you. He's greater than any sickness and disease, and He is greater than lack and poverty.

There will be times when the pain is great, when the fear sucks the air out of the room, and you don't feel God is near. The midnight hour comes to all of us; we are not immune to the challenges of life just because we are Christians. You may not feel like the spirit of a conqueror lives in you, but go forward in faith anyway.

The Bible tells us, "Many are the afflictions of the righteous, but God delivers them out of them all."

Regardless of what you feel, God is with you and will see you through. So, when you are facing that impossible task, look yourself in the mirror and remind yourself that the undaunted and unconquerable Spirit of God is within you. So lean on the Greater One. Activate His help through speaking the Word of God, and trust in him with an unwavering heart! Stop comparing yourself to the giant of a problem you are faced with, and instead compare the problem to the giant of a God who lives within you. No matter how great the problem is, He is greater still.

Scriptures

And what agreement has the temple of God with idols? For you are the temple of the living God. As God has said: "I will dwell in them and walk among them. I will be their God, and they shall be my people."

–2 Corinthians 6:16 (NKJV)

My dear children, you come from God and belong to God. You have already won a big victory over those false teachers, for the Spirit in you is far stronger than anything in the world.

–1 John 4:4 (MSG)

What shall we then say to these things? If God be for us, who can be against us?

–Romans 8:31 (KJV)

If anyone acknowledges that Jesus is the Son of God, God lives in them and they in God. And so we know and rely on the love God has for us.

–1 John 4:15-16a (NIV)

Speak These Words Over Your Life

Greater is He that is in me than he that is in the world. He is greater than any crisis I might face. He is greater than any storm that may arise. He is greater than any problem or difficulty in my life. He gives me the strength, courage, and fortitude to overcome. He gives me wisdom and supernatural direction to pursue God's plan for my life with confidence.

God is for me, He is with me, and He is on my side. The Creator of the universe, the shaper of all things, and my personal Savior is living in me. I will not fear in times of trouble. I will not magnify my problems; I will magnify God. No weapon formed against me will prosper. When my strength and endurance have reached their limit, I will lean on the Greater One, knowing that His strength will carry me through.

Chapter 8

I Have a Protector

Every day there are reports of shootings, terrorist attacks, and unfathomable crimes committed against innocent people. Sickness and disease run rampant. Tragedy and peril seem to be lurking around every corner. If we are not careful, it is easy to become fearful and anxious about our safety and the safety of our loved ones.

But I have good news! Part of the benefits and privileges of being a Christian is God's promise of protection for us and our family. One of the greatest passages on God's promise of protection for you, His child, can be found in the 91st Psalm. Read it, let His promise fill your heart with confidence and peace. Release the power of His words in your life by speaking them over yourself and your family. As we truly make Him our refuge, we can depend on and trust in His protection.

"You who sit down in the High God's presence, spend the night in Shaddai's shadow, Say this: "God, you're my refuge. I trust in you and I'm safe! That's right—he rescues you from hidden traps, shields you from deadly hazards. His huge outstretched arms protect you—under them you're perfectly safe; his arms fend off all harm. Fear nothing—not wild wolves in the night, not flying arrows in the day, Not disease that prowls through the darkness, not disaster that erupts at high noon. Even though others succumb all around, drop like flies right and left, no harm will even graze you. You'll stand untouched, watch it all from a distance, watch the wicked turn into corpses. Yes, because God's your refuge, the High God your very own home, Evil can't get close to you, harm can't get through the door. He ordered his angels to guard you wherever you go. If you stumble, they'll catch you; their job is to keep you from falling. You'll walk unharmed among lions and snakes, and kick young lions and serpents from the path." Psalm 91:1-13 (MSG)

Scriptures

But the Lord is faithful, and He will strengthen you setting you on a firm foundation and will protect *and* guard you from the evil *one*.

–2 THESSALONIANS 3:3 (AMP)

God is a safe place to hide, ready to help when we need him. We stand fearless at the cliff-edge of doom, courageous in seastorm and earthquake, Before the rush and roar of oceans, the tremors that shift mountains.

–PSALM 46:1-3 (MSG)

The Lord is my Shepherd to feed, to guide and to shield me, I shall not want.

–PSALM 23:1 (AMP)

Even though I walk through the sunless valley of the shadow of death, I fear no evil, for You are with me; Your rod to protect and Your staff to guide, they comfort *and* console me.

–PSALM 23:4 (AMP)

Speak These Words Over Your Life

My family and I walk in complete and total protection from harm, evil, danger, and accidents of any kind. I refuse to live in fear. I will not worry or become anxious regarding our safety because I put my trust and confidence in God. I purpose to make Him my refuge and enjoy the promise of safety that comes with that position. I know He will keep us safe from danger and destruction. I am sensitive to the voice of the Holy Spirit and quick to obey His direction regarding the safety and well-being of my family.

Chapter 9

I Have Peace

It seems like we are all continually searching for more peace in our lives. Our peace is under constant attack. The flow of text messages, emails, calls and more from friends, family, and people we don't even know; the daily grind of work and everyday living; and the challenges that life throws at us on a regular basis can stress us out to the point where there is no peace left in our lives.

But is peace just the lack of feeling stressed, tired, or anxious? Can it be gained by a quiet evening, reading a novel, or watching a favorite show on TV? Maybe temporarily, but that kind of peace is fleeting and dissipates the moment you step back into the real world. When Jesus left this earth after being resurrected, He said this:

"Peace I leave with you, my peace I give unto you: not as the world giveth, give I unto you. Let not your heart be troubled, neither let it be afraid." John 14:27

Our minds and emotions can't comprehend how we can be calm, cool, and collected in the middle of the craziness of life. This is not the world's fleeting peace gained from external leisure but rather an everlasting peace that comes from our trust in God. In Isaiah 26, God says, "I will keep them in perfect peace whose eyes are fixed on me."

If you need more peace in your life, then maybe you need to change where you are looking. Peace is not the absence of problems. Peace is the state of a child of God who is self-assured because of their faith in Him, which means you can be full of peace even in the middle of a major crisis. Your joy and peace of mind are never at the mercy of your circumstances. When you choose to look to God and trust Him to take care of you and sustain you, then the busyness of life will cease to overwhelm you and His peace will bring you to a state of calmness and joy that can only come from Him.

Worry, fear, and anxiety say, "What if…", but peace smiles and says, "God will."

Scriptures

"The Lord will give strength unto his people; the Lord will bless his people with peace."

–PSALM 29:11 (KJV)

"May the God of hope fill you with all joy and peace as you trust in him, so that you may overflow with hope by the power of the Holy Spirit."

–ROMANS 15:13 (NIV)

"Do not be anxious or worried about anything, but in everything [every circumstance and situation] by prayer and petition with thanksgiving, continue to make your [specific] requests known to God. And the peace of God [that peace which reassures the heart, that peace] which transcends all understanding, [that peace which] stands guard over your hearts and your minds in Christ Jesus [is yours]."

–PHILIPPIANS 4:6-7 (AMP)

Speak These Words Over Your Life

I have peace that passes all understanding. I can face any problem or challenge in my life without getting fretful, disturbed, or anxious. I refuse to let fear run rampant in my life. I refuse to let the busyness of everyday life stress me out. I refuse to let the constant pressures of this life push me to the edge. And I refuse to fall victim to my own thoughts and emotions. I will not be distraught or frustrated when unexpected glitches or difficulties pop up in my life. In the midst of trying times, I will find rest and peace in the presence of the Almighty. I will not turn my eyes from God no matter the intensity of the storm I find myself in, for He is my source of peace. I will not become agitated because of what other people say or do. I will keep my mind at peace and my heart steady when I am tempted to worry or become fearful because I put my trust in God. His peace gives me assurance that everything will work out for my good.

Chapter 10

I Have the Holy Spirit

The Holy Spirit is the source of power and strength which Jesus operated in while here on the earth. After His resurrection, Jesus promised that God would send the Holy Spirit to live in us as our supernatural resource for every area of life. Many think the Holy Spirit is some mystical, mysterious force that is flighty and unpredictable.

This is not the case; the Bible specifically tells us the roles that the Holy Spirit fulfills in our lives. He works in us, for us, and through us to fulfill the plan of God in our lives.

He is our Helper, forever lending support to those who ask God for help.

He is the Spirit of God. Your body acts as a temple to house His presence, so your spirit can commune with God. God speaks to us, through His spirit, by revealing the truth of the Bible and by wisdom spoken to our hearts. Our ability to hear His voice is enhanced in our time spent with the Lord in prayer and worship.

He is our Comforter. When life gets tough, He'll take us to the words that God has spoken to you—words of love, words of affirmation, words of strength, words of freedom, and words of hope.

He's our Counselor, helping us navigate life. He guides us to a place of peace and joy using the Word of God as a map for finding balance between work, play, relationships, and rest. He'll supply you with wisdom and guidance.

The Holy Spirit is here to help us. Many have tried to live life fighting all its storms, all their impure desires, and all their problems by themselves when help is available to us. The Bible puts it like this in Romans 8:5-6:

"Those who think they can do it on their own end up obsessed with measuring their own moral muscle but never get around to exercising it in real life. Those who trust God's action in them find that God's Spirit is in them—living and breathing God! Obsession with self in these matters is a dead end; attention to God leads us out into the open, into a spacious, free life." (MSG)

Scriptures

But the Helper (Comforter, Advocate, Intercessor—Counselor, Strengthener, Standby), the Holy Spirit, whom the Father will send in My name [in My place, to represent Me and act on My behalf], He will teach you all things. And He will help you remember everything that I have told you.

–John 14:26 (AMP)

Then Peter said unto them, Repent, and be baptized every one of you in the name of Jesus Christ for the remission of sins, and ye shall receive the gift of the Holy Ghost.

–Acts 2:38 (KJV)

Don't you realize that your body is the temple of the Holy Spirit, who lives in you and was given to you by God? You do not belong to yourself.

–1 Corinthians 6:19 (NLT)

Speak These Words Over Your Life

I have the Holy Spirit living in me. The same Spirit that raised Christ Jesus from the dead lives in me, revitalizing and infusing my body with strength. And the Holy Spirit is working in me and through me to fulfill God's plan for my life. He is my Helper, He is my Comfort, and He is my Guide. He reveals the truths and insights in God's Word. As I study and meditate on the Scriptures, He gives me wisdom and understanding. When I am facing a critical decision, He gives me wisdom, strength, and courage to face any adversity or challenge life sends my way.

Chapter 11

I Have Authority and Dominion

You have authority and dominion as God's representative on this earth. Jesus operated in divine authority on this earth because He did His miracles through God's direction. Jesus said in John the 14th chapter,

That He did and said nothing lest He heard His father say it first.

Consequently, when Jesus exercised His authority to perform God's will on the earth, He looked within and sought the words that God would have Him speak over His current situation. He spoke those words with faith in God and confidence in His position as God's representative.

According to God's ultimate plan of redemption for us, through the death and resurrection of Jesus Christ, we were saved and have become Christ's ambassadors, equipped with His authority and dominion. Jesus himself tells us,

"Behold, I have given you authority to tread on serpents and scorpions, and over all the power of the enemy, and nothing shall hurt you." Luke 10:19 (ESV)

This doesn't mean you should look for snakes to step on or put yourself in a dangerous situation to prove something. God gives us wisdom, and if there is a way to avoid calamity, then we need to exercise that wisdom. The reason for your authority is for your protection—you are never to be powerless or a victim of circumstances or subdued by the power of the enemy. You are to walk confidently in faith. We are equipped and empowered to operate as Jesus did; He even said in the 14th chapter of John,

"Whoever believes in me will also do the works that I do; and greater works than these will he do, because I am going to the Father."

This doesn't seem possible, and in fact if Jesus didn't say it, then it would be difficult to believe. But He *did* say it, so you need never to shirk in fear or doubt when faced with impossible odds because you are a child of the Most High God! Jesus has bestowed upon us power and authority to walk in dominion while on this earth.

So, activate your authority by speaking the words of God in faith over your circumstances. Be secure in your position, and remember your authority—then speak out His words with faith in and through the delegated authority of Jesus Christ.

Scriptures

Then God said, "Let us make man in our image, after our likeness. And let them have dominion over the fish of the sea and over the birds of the heavens and over the livestock and over all the earth and over every creeping thing that creeps on the earth."

–GENESIS 1:26 (ESV)

Now you understand that I have imparted to you all my authority to trample over his kingdom. You will trample upon every demon before you and overcome every power Satan possesses. Absolutely nothing will be able to harm you as you walk in this authority.

–LUKE 10:19 (TPT)

What are mere mortals that you should think about them, human beings that you should care for them? Yet you made them only a little lower than God and crowned them with glory and honor. You gave them charge of everything you made, putting all things under their authority

–PSALMS 8:4-6 (NLT)

Speak These Words Over Your Life

As God's ambassador and representative on this earth, I have dominion and authority to walk in total victory. The enemy has no power to bring destruction or calamity to my life. I walk and live with bold and confident faith. I am a victor, not a victim. I have learned to rise above the adverse circumstances of life. I am a joint heir with Jesus and enjoy the rights and privileges promised to me in God's Word.

Chapter 12

I Have Provision

Let there be no mistake or misconception about God's love for you—your needs touches Him. He is not indifferent concerning your affairs. He loves you and cares about you. He wants you to live a blessed and fulfilled life. Being in lack is not God's will for your life.

If you are going through some financial challenges right now, don't be discouraged. This is not indicative of God's disapproval or His will. God wants you to be successful. Even if your poor choices are the reason you are experiencing financial difficulties, God hasn't given up on you, so ask for His forgiveness and move on in His mercy and grace. Then, read His promises concerning your provision, speak them over your life, and thank God for His help. Choose to look more at His Word and less at the bills and your bank account. Dwell on His provision instead of your lack. Magnify God instead of the problem.

God is your Father, so ask Him if there is anything you should be doing differently and He will guide you in the way you should go.

Your debt may be forgiven, you may get a promotion at work to cover the difference, you may have an idea that produces a profit for your family, or opportunities may present themselves for you to earn extra income. It's up to Him how your provision comes, but it's up to you to believe that it's coming. Hear Jesus' thoughts about God's provision from His own mouth:

"If God gives such attention to the appearance of wildflowers—most of which are never even seen—don't you think he'll attend to you, take pride in you, do his best for you? What I'm trying to do here is to get you to relax, to not be so preoccupied with getting, so you can respond to God's giving. People who don't know God and the way he works fuss over these things, but you know both God and how he works. Steep your life in God-reality, God-initiative, God-provisions. Don't worry about missing out. You'll find all your everyday human concerns will be met."

–MATTHEW 6:30-33 (MSG)

Scriptures

But my God shall supply all your need according to his riches in glory by Christ Jesus.

–PHILIPPIANS 4:19 (KJV)

If you remain in Me and My words remain in you [that is, if we are vitally united and My message lives in your heart], ask whatever you wish and it will be done for you.

–JOHN 15:7 (AMP)

The blessing of the Lord makes a person rich, and he adds no sorrow with it.

–PROVERBS 10:22 (NLT)

The Lord is my shepherd, I lack nothing.

–PSALM 23:1 (NIV)

Now to Him Who, by (in consequence of) the [action of His] power that is at work within us, is able to [carry out His purpose and] do superabundantly, far over and above all that we [dare] ask or think [infinitely beyond our highest prayers, desires, thoughts, hopes, or dreams].

–EPHESIANS 3:20 (AMPC)

Speak These Words Over Your Life

The Lord is my Provider, and He will supply all my needs. He loves me, cares about me, and wants me to succeed in life. He wants me to have a blessed and fulfilled life. He gives me wisdom and insight on how to manage my finances successfully. He gives me favor concerning financial transactions. He gives me creative ideas on how to increase my income. I declare all my bills paid. My debts are being reduced and eliminated. I am a child of the Most High God. It is not His will for me to have lack or live under financial stress. He provides me with multiple streams of income. I declare I shall have more than enough money each month to cover all my obligations and plenty left over to give to the Kingdom and the welfare of others.

Chapter 13

I Have the Promise of Healing and a Long Life

Health and healing are available to every Christian. It is a gift from God! God is a good God, and He sent Jesus to the earth to save His kids—not just from spiritual death but also from physical pain and torment! Jesus never denied anyone healing in the Bible who asked Him for it. The Bible puts it like this in Acts: *"God anointed Jesus of Nazareth with the Holy Spirit and power, and how **he went around doing good and healing all** who were under the power of the devil, because God was with him."*

The Bible also says that Jesus is the same yesterday, today, and forever, which means He's still in the healing business. Jesus loves you very much and wants you to be healthy and whole so that you can live life to the fullest! He said it Himself in the 10th chapter of John:

*"The thief comes only to steal and kill and destroy; **I have come that they may have life, and have it to the full.**"*

God was with Jesus, and it was God through Jesus who caused the healing to manifest on this earth. It is God's will for you to be healed. There is a name that God was called in the Bible, "*Jehovah Rapha,*" which means,

"*I am the God that Heals.*"

God is not the author of sickness and diseases; He is the healer of them. He gave us His Word, which is filled with faith, life, and the promise of healing. It is through His words that God sends His healing.

"He sent out his word and healed them, snatching them from the door of death." Psalm 107:20 (NLT)

His Word is alive, and there is life in it to heal you. If you will meditate on His words and believe in Him, then the same life that is in the Word of God will come into you.

"My child, pay attention to what I say. Listen carefully to my words. Don't lose sight of them. Let them penetrate deep into your heart, for they bring life to those who find them, and healing to their whole body." Proverbs 4:20-22 (NLT)

Let His words penetrate deep into your heart and accept the gift of life and healing in them!

Scriptures

He was despised and rejected—a man of sorrows, acquainted with deepest grief. We turned our backs on him and looked the other way. He was despised, and we did not care. Yet it was our weaknesses he carried; it was our sorrows that weighed him down. And we thought his troubles were a punishment from God, a punishment for his own sins! But he was pierced for our rebellion, crushed for our sins. He was beaten so we could be whole. He was whipped so we could be healed.

–ISAIAH 53:3-5 (NLT)

"Are you weary, carrying a heavy burden? Then come to me. I will refresh your life, for I am your oasis.

–MATTHEW 11:28 (TPT)

He personally carried our sins in His body on the cross willingly offering Himself on it, as on an altar of sacrifice, so that we might die to sin becoming immune from the penalty and power of sin and live for righteousness; for by His wounds you who believe have been healed.

–1 PETER 2:24 (AMP)

Speak These Words Over Your Life

I call my body strong, healthy, healed, and whole, free from sickness and disease. I am full of divine life and vitality. I declare every system in my body operates precisely the way God designed it to. I declare every organ and gland in my body is healthy and whole and functions at maximum efficiency. I declare my bones are strong. I declare my body is free from growths, tumors, cysts, and cancers. I declare my blood is healthy and free from disease or unhealthy cells. My immune system is strong and resilient. My sight is strong, and my hearing is clear. The life of God in me sustains me and keeps me healthy.

Chapter 14

I Have a Way Out

Sometimes we may find ourselves in a situation where it looks like there is no way out. The problem is too big, the odds are stacked against us, and it seems like there is no way to climb out. Fear and worry may have driven you to discouragement and despair. But don't be dismayed, I have good news for you! With Jesus, there is always a way out. There is not a hole so deep that He is unable to pull you out of it! If you are lost and confused, He'll find you. If you are weary and tired, He'll strengthen you. If you are dry and broken, He'll refresh you and supply you.

He said it Himself: "I am the Way." He is your way out of every adverse circumstance. He is the way you break free from worry, fear, and depression. He is the way to a loving relationship with your Father, God. He is the way to eternal life. You have Him in your life as your Friend and Advocate! Instead of leaning on your own strength, lean on Him. Let His Word bolster your faith in Christ and spur you on towards victory.

It's not time to lie down; it's time to rise up! It's not time to withdraw; it's time to advance! It's not time to give up; it's time to fight back! Through His Word and the guidance of the Holy Spirit, He sets a path of deliverance before you. Ask God about your part and then trust Him to do what you can't. Whether the Lord delivers you "from" a trial or "through" a trial, know that He is with you to provide courage, strength, and endurance.

So, quit magnifying the problem and start magnifying the solution, Jesus Christ. Start thanking God for your deliverance right in the middle of your trial. There is no stronger proclamation of faith than thanksgiving for help while you see no signs of change.

So, keep believing, keep trusting in His promises to you, be willing to play your role in your deliverance, and you will see the other side of the trial.

Scriptures

"If you'll hold on to me for dear life," says God, "I'll get you out of any trouble. I'll give you the best of care if you'll only get to know and trust me. Call me and I'll answer, be at your side in bad times; I'll rescue you, then throw you a party. I'll give you a long life, give you a long drink of salvation!"

–PSALM 91:14-16 (MSG)

For the Lord is the Spirit, and wherever the Spirit of the Lord is, there is freedom.

–2 CORINTHIANS 3:17 (NLT)

But I'll take the hand of those who don't know the way, who can't see where they're going. I'll be a personal guide to them, directing them through unknown country. I'll be right there to show them what roads to take, make sure they don't fall into the ditch. These are the things I'll be doing for them—sticking with them, not leaving them for a minute."

–ISAIAH 42:16 (MSG)

Jesus saith unto him, I am the way, the truth, and the life: no man cometh unto the Father, but by me.

–JOHN 14:6 (KJV)

Speak These Words Over Your Life

I will not fear when I feel the pressures of this world constricting me, for I know that they cannot crush me. I will not fall into despair when I can't figure things out. I will not be anxious or intimidated; instead, I will put my trust in God. I know He will bring me out. I declare that there is no such thing as a hopeless situation with God. I will not panic when faced with what seems to be impossible odds, because I know that what is impossible with man is possible with God. I will not distress if I make a mistake or if a crisis arises because I know that with God there is always a way out. God gives me clarity of thought and wisdom to handle my situation. I'm never forsaken, never left to fend for myself, and never will I stand alone against the attacks of this world!

Chapter 15

I Have Faith

Faith is the key that opens the door to all of God's blessings, the catalyst that produces an environment for the miraculous to manifest in your life. Faith is essential to receiving what God has promised us. The Bible defines faith like this:

"Now faith is the assurance (the confirmation, the title deed) of the things we hope for, being the proof of things we do not see and the conviction of their reality. faith perceiving as real fact what is not revealed to the senses." (Hebrews 11:1 AMPC)

The Bible further tells us that God has given every believer "*a measure of faith.*" This means you have the ability to believe in something you can't see but you know in your heart is true anyway. That's how you became a Christian! It is up to you to grow the faith you have been given. Growing your faith is simple—you have to feed it and exercise it.

You feed your faith by reading the Word of God. As you take time to get to know God personally through His Word, faith will come alive in your heart. When you read and meditate on God's promises, your faith will grow stronger and stronger. Your knowledge of who God is, what He has already done for you, and what He has promised will begin to expand. This process creates an intimacy with God that causes our faith in Him to flourish.

You exercise your faith by believing in what God said in His Word regardless of how adverse your circumstances are and then by activating the Word of God by speaking it over your life. When the Bible says one thing, and you are experiencing another thing, faith chooses to trust that your circumstances will conform to what the Bible says. Choose to focus on the Word of God more than your circumstance, choose to see that God is bigger than your problem, choose to speak His words instead of fear and doubt, and you have the guarantee of God that your circumstances will conform to what He has promised you.

Scriptures

Because of the grace that God gave me, I can say to each one of you: don't think of yourself more highly than you ought to think. Instead, be reasonable since God has measured out a portion of faith to each one of you.

–ROMANS 12:3 (CEB)

Now faith is the assurance (the confirmation, the title deed) of the things we hope for, being the proof of things we do not see *and* the conviction of their reality faith perceiving as real fact what is not revealed to the senses.

–HEBREWS 11:1 (AMPC)

For whatsoever is born of God overcometh the world: and this is the victory that overcometh the world, even our faith.

–1 JOHN 5:4 (KJV)

But without faith it is impossible to please him: for he that cometh to God must believe that he is, and that he is a rewarder of them that diligently seek him.

–HEBREWS 11:6 (KJV)

Speak These Words Over Your Life

I have faith in God's Word. I put my trust and confidence in Him. I walk by faith and not by sight. I choose to trust in the Lord no matter what comes my way. Even in the midst of difficulties and challenges, I have faith that God will not let me down or abandon me. As I study and meditate on His words, my faith grows stronger and stronger. My faith is in God, not in my ability, not in others, and not in the government. It is only in my God. By faith, I will overcome any challenges life throws at me. By faith, I will fulfill God's purpose and destiny for my life.

Chapter 16

I Have Wisdom and Guidance

Our decisions define and shape our lives. Who you are today is the product of choices you have made in the past, and the choices you make today will decide your future. This is why it is so critical that we learn how to follow God's lead in our lives; it takes all the stress, fear, and anxiety out of our lives and replaces it with peace and purpose.

Being guided by God sounds mystical, as if you were going to hear a thundering voice from heaven that tells you what you need to do. It's much less spectacular than that but no less powerful. God leads us through wisdom and peace. His wisdom comes from three major sources: the leading of the Holy Spirit, His Word, and the godly counsel of others. The Bible says in Colossians,

"And let the peace (soul harmony which comes) from Christ rule (act as umpire continually) in your hearts deciding and settling with finality all questions that arise in your minds, in

that peaceful state to which as members of Christ's one body you were also called to live. And be thankful (appreciative), giving praise to God always."

When you trust God with your life and live in His peace, you'll be able to discern the best decision. God will provide you with wisdom if you just ask for it. The Bible puts it like this:

"If any of you lacks wisdom to guide him through a decision or circumstance, he is to ask of our benevolent God, who gives to everyone generously and without rebuke or blame, and it will be given to him."

If the wisdom is from God, we will have peace about acting upon that wisdom. God genuinely wants the best for your life. He wants you to be joyful, at peace, and full of confidence knowing that you are fulfilling the purpose that He has specifically chosen for you. So whether you have a big decision to make or a small one, lean on God for wisdom and guidance, because if it matters to you, it matters to Him.

Scriptures

"If any of you lacks wisdom [to guide him through a decision or circumstance], he is to ask of [our benevolent] God, who gives to everyone generously and without rebuke *or* blame, and it will be given to him."

–JAMES 1:5 (AMP)

"But the wisdom that comes from heaven is first of all pure; then peace-loving, considerate, submissive, full of mercy and good fruit, impartial and sincere."

–JAMES 3:17 (NIV)

And let the peace (soul harmony which comes) from Christ rule (act as umpire continually) in your hearts [deciding and settling with finality all questions that arise in your minds, in that peaceful state] to which as [members of Christ's] one body you were also called [to live]. And be thankful (appreciative), [giving praise to God always].

–COLOSSIANS 3:15 (AMPC)

Thus says the Lord, your Redeemer, the Holy One of Israel: "I am the Lord your God, who teaches you to profit, who leads you in the way you should go."

–ISAIAH 48:17 (ESV)

Speak These Words Over Your Life

By the Spirit of the Lord and through God's words, I receive His wisdom for every area of my life. By His Spirit, He leads and guides me in the fulfillment of His perfect will. He gives me direction and insight concerning any decisions I need to make. He gives me clarity of thought and discernment when faced with perplexing situations. He gives me sound and accurate judgement when considering options that require my input. I declare that because I walk in God's wisdom, His peace is the anchor for my soul.

Chapter 17

I Have Victory

Even though we are Christians, there is no question that we will face challenges and difficulties in life. The Bible even tells us that *"Many are the afflictions of the righteous but the Lord delivers them out of them all."*

You may get a few scrapes and bruises along the way, but if you trust in God, cling to His Word, and refuse to give into despair, you will overcome. Your situation might feel hopeless, and it might look like there is no way out, but with God's help you can and you will overcome anything!

Everyone's needs and desires are different. But whatever you specifically need to achieve your goals, to see your dreams realized, to overcome an addiction, or to make it through a crisis—whatever it may be—God is your answer.

God did not promise us that we would never have any problems in our lives, but He did promise us the victory over them. You may be knocked down by trouble, but with God's strength you can get back up again. You may feel perplexed or distraught, but there is no need to worry because God will give you the wisdom to see you through any situation. You may feel under pressure, but there is no need to be anxious when God is with you and for you.

God's will for your life is total victory—victory in every area of your life. Victory over the powers of darkness, victory over any adversity, and victory over any obstacle that would keep you from achieving your God-given destiny. The Bible tells us that through the Lord, we are more than conquerors—we are world overcomers.

Christ is living in you, and He overcame sin, all the power of the enemy, and even death itself! So, victory is part of your spiritual DNA. God created you by and for complete and total victory! Let go of your fear, worry, and anxiety and let Him strengthen you, encourage you, and lead you in His peace to a place of victory.

With God, your future is secure and your victory assured.

Scriptures

But thanks be to God! He gives us the victory through our Lord Jesus Christ.

–1 CORINTHIANS 15:57 (NIV)

Now thanks be unto God, which **always** causeth us to triumph in Christ, and maketh manifest the savour of his knowledge by us in every place.

–2 CORINTHIANS 2:14 (KJV)

We are hedged in (pressed) on every side troubled and oppressed in every way, but not cramped *or* crushed; we suffer embarrassments *and* are perplexed *and* unable to find a way out, but not driven to despair; We are pursued (persecuted and hard driven), but not deserted to stand alone; we are struck down to the ground, but never struck out *and* destroyed;

–2 CORINTHIANS 4:8-9 (AMPC)

Speak These Words Over Your Life

I have the victory!!! I am a champion of God, I am a child of the Most High, I am an ambassador for His Kingdom, I have Jesus Christ as my advocate, and I have a portion of the same spiritual substance that God used to frame the world: Faith, both as a shield and a sword to protect and fight back against any and all attacks of the enemy.

I am strong in the Lord and the power of His might. I am a victor, not a victim. I am more than a conqueror through my Lord Jesus Christ. I am a world overcomer. I will arise above every challenge that confronts me. I will boldly and confidently meet every adversity with undaunted faith.

My victory is as sure as the Word of God, which is my foundation. I will run my race, reach the goals God has put before me, fulfill my calling, and I shall have victory in every area of my life.

Chapter 18

I Have the Armor of God

You alone are not strong enough to withstand all the problems and trials that you face in life by yourself. That is why God makes His armor available to every Christian. It is His answer to the attacks of the enemy. It is up to you to wear it and use it!

You fasten the Belt of Truth by allowing the Word of God to be the final authority in your life—by living your life according to its principles, by transforming your words, actions, and by conforming your very perspective to the Word of God. The Bible is truth, and by using it as your belt, you hold the rest of your armor in the correct place.

You equip the Breastplate of Righteousness by accepting Jesus' sacrifice as a sufficient punishment for any mistake you've made—or will make. You protect the love in your heart by accepting His great love for you, which negates your enemy's attempt at condemnation.

Strap on your feet the shoes of the Gospel of Peace. They give you firm footing and stability in the Spirit, allowing you to advance through life in the Lord's strength and not your own, with your eyes firmly fixed on the Lord. God said, "I will keep him in perfect peace whose mind is fixed on me."

Raise your Shield of Faith by choosing to look at God's Word instead of the circumstances in your life. Walk by faith, and not by sight. Raise the shield by choosing to unwaveringly trust in God, knowing He will never leave you or forsake you. He shall deliver you from all the attacks of the enemy!

Put on the Helmet of Salvation. You have been saved from a life fated for destruction and have been adopted into the kingdom of light and have access to all the rights and privileges that go with that position, so recognize that Jesus' sacrifice is your salvation. He died and rose again so that God could remake you from head to toe.

And finally, draw your Sword of the Spirit! It's God's Spirit of dynamite power, which is the spoken Word of God. Face every adversity with the confidence and determination of a conqueror who has the assurance of total victory!

Scriptures

[13] Therefore put on God's complete armor, that you may be able to resist *and* stand your ground on the evil day [of danger], and, having done all [the crisis demands], to stand [firmly in your place].

[14] Stand therefore [hold your ground], having tightened the belt of truth around your loins and having put on the breastplate of integrity *and* of moral rectitude *and* right standing with God,

[15] And having shod your feet in preparation [to face the enemy with the firm-footed stability, the promptness, and the readiness produced by the good news] of the Gospel of peace.

[16] Lift up over all the [covering] shield of saving faith, upon which you can quench all the flaming missiles of the wicked [one].

[17] And take the helmet of salvation and the sword that the Spirit wields, which is the Word of God.

–EPHESIANS 6:13-18 (AMPC)

Speak These Words Over Your Life

I have the spiritual armor of God at my disposal. I choose to put on my armor today. I am more than a conqueror, and I can do all things through Christ who strengthens me. With God's armor on, I am invincible. I am ready for anything and equal to anything that life throws my way. By His Spirit and through His Word I shall be victorious in every challenge I face. God's Word is the final authority in my life. Its truth and principles are my foundation and protect my heart. I will govern my thoughts and actions according to its direction. I know that Jesus' sacrifice assures my forgiveness and wipes the slate clean and I have now been redeemed from sin and the destructive forces of evil. I will advance in life with His peace leading the way. I will not be moved by what I see or deterred by what I feel; instead I will walk by faith, trusting in God's unfailing love and faithfulness. God's armor equips me with all I need to live a life of victory and fulfill my God-given destiny.

I CAN

DO WHAT THE BIBLE SAYS I CAN DO

Introduction

Most Christians live far below the level of fulfillment, joy, and quality of life that God desires for them. But that is not what God intended! It is essential for us to come to the realization that, through our relationship with Christ and by the power of God's Word, *we can do all things.* Anything He has told us to do, He provides along with the directive, the grace, empowerment, equipment, and help necessary to do it!

God sent His very own Spirit to dwell within us to empower, comfort, and guide us into the life He had always planned for us to have. We have the same Spirit that raised Christ from the dead living in us! The Christian condition is not a life of survival, barely making it through day by day. We are called to live a life of Faith, aggressively advancing under fire towards our God given destiny, with God's Word as the anchor for our souls, utilizing the gifts afforded to us as God's children, and depending on the Holy Spirit leadings and empowerments!

God never promised that the life of a believer would be one without challenges. He did promise the power and companionship to face these challenges head on—and to triumph over them. We are called, equipped, and supernaturally empowered to change our lives—and have a powerful impact on the lives of others.

We are sons and daughters of the Almighty God; we are not to look for pity and act like victims in our own lives. When the storm winds blow, a greater intimacy with our Father God will be forged as we trust in and rely on Him. When we find ourselves in the fiery crucible of crisis, we can be confident knowing that our faith is going to be tested, strengthened, and purified as we esteem the Word of God higher than life's greatest challenges. There is nothing this life can throw at us that we can't overcome! We are called to rise above life's difficulties with an unshakeable faith in God. A faith that comes from an uncompromising conviction in the never-failing, life-empowering, bondage-breaking, life-giving, and faith-producing nature of the Word of God. God's words are *alive,* and His commands and encouragements carry with them immeasurable power. It's time to tap into this power and elevate your perception, ability, and quality of life to the level God destined for you.

I encourage you to read on and let God heal your past, empower your present, and clarify your future. **It is time to do what the Bible says you can do.**

I Can Transform My Life

You have the power to transform your life completely. Do you want to go from victim to victor, from a failure to a success, from fearful to peaceful? You can go from depressed to joyful, from insecure to confident, from confusion to clarity, from being trapped to being set free! The Bible calls this transformation process "renewing your mind." When you were born again, your spirit was reborn, but your mind was not.

Renewing your mind is exactly what you'd expect—the process of retraining the way you think. Your mind is the result of all of your experiences—good and bad—up to this point. Your experiences have shaped a large part of who you are. However, you are more than what has happened to you; you are a child of God. God wonderfully crafted you, and He placed passions, gifts, talents, and a fulfilling purpose in you that He wants to accomplish—not *for* you but *through* you.

Renewing your mind is choosing to identify with who *God* says you are instead of what others have said, what your past says, or even what your present circumstances say about you. You renew your mind by reading and meditating on the Scriptures—God's living message to you—and focusing on all that God has done for you and in you. Instead of flooding your eyes and ears with the corruption of this world, you immerse yourself in God's Word.

God is our Abba Father, and when you renew your mind, you adopt the way He sees you, accept the gifts that He has given you, and accomplish the things He said you can do! God created you and placed all your talents, passions, and dreams inside you. He knows exactly who you are and what you can do. It takes faith to hold on to what He says you are, what He says you have, and what He says you can do when your experiences tell you something entirely different.

That's why the process of renewing your mind is a daily one; you are constantly keeping a guard over what you watch and listen to, and, ultimately, what you think about. As we do this, day by day, we begin to transform into the happiest version of ourselves—the joyful, peaceful, and confident version that God always intended us to be. As we exchange our past for His promise, our dreams, passion, and purpose become more evident, and our love for God grows along with our desire to please Him.

Scriptures

Do not be conformed to this world (this age), fashioned after and adapted to its external, superficial customs, but be transformed (changed) by the entire renewal of your mind by its new ideals and its new attitude, so that you may prove for yourselves what is the good and acceptable and perfect will of God, even the thing which is good and acceptable and perfect in His sight for you.

–ROMANS 12:2 (AMPC)

Therefore if any man be in Christ, he is a new creature: old things are passed away; behold, all things are become new.

–2 CORINTHIANS 5:17 (KJV)

And he has taught you to let go of the lifestyle of the ancient man, the old self - life, which was corrupted by sinful and deceitful desires that spring from delusions. Now it's time to be made new by every revelation that's been given to you. And to be transformed as you embrace the glorious Christ-within as your new life and live in union with him! For God has re-created you all over again in his perfect righteousness, and you now belong to him in the realm of true holiness.

–EPHESIANS 4:22-24 (TPT)

Speak these words over your life:

I am being transformed daily. My thoughts, actions, and emotions are being shaped by the Word of God. I rely on the Lord for answers to the questions that arise in my life, and I refuse to depend on the wisdom of the world. I am growing in wisdom and stature as I absorb and act on the truth of God's Word. I will not be influenced by the problems, tests, or any crisis that comes my way. I will remain firmly planted and established in the integrity of God's Word. My perspective is becoming more godly day by day as I gain clarity and understanding as I apply the transforming principles found in God's Word. As my mind is being transformed, I am becoming more spiritually aware of God's plan and purpose for my life and increasing in my ability to believe and act according to His will for my life. I value and honor the gift of God's Word, and I will keep it in the highest place, as the final authority, in my life.

I Can Beat Addiction

This may shock you, but you were *created* to be *addicted*.

As we grow up in the natural, we should grow more and more *independent*. But as we grow up spiritually, we are to grow more and more *dependent*—on God. We develop a longing for His presence and rely more and more on His direction, peace, and joy.

God created us to be His kids and to live addicted to being with Him—His presence. He wanted us to always know the elation and satisfaction of living in a genuine relationship with our Heavenly Father. However, Satan has designed cheap "knock-offs" that try to serve as substitutes for living in close connection with God, and they are powerful weapons designed to steal your passion and dull your effectiveness.

Most know their addiction is harmful, whether it is drugs, alcohol, smoking, pornography, gambling, or a myriad of other things. Accepting its destructive nature is not the issue; we feel desperate and helpless when we try to overcome our addictions. You may have read every book you could find, prayed a thousand prayers, joined support groups, and done anything else you could think of. Or you may be in the midst of an internal war, living a double life where you feel more isolated with every relationship and every positive interaction, because they are complimenting or trying to connect with who you are *pretending* to be, and not the "real" you. Addictions always isolate, and eventually all who struggle with such things come to the same conclusion—"I can't beat this thing."

The truth is, that's exactly right. You alone cannot beat addiction, and you probably feel you aren't strong or disciplined enough to overcome.

But I have good news: *you are not alone*, and you never will be alone. God is with you, God is in you, God is for you, and He is on your side. With His help, you *will* overcome! The Bible says if you walk in the Spirit you will not gratify your fleshly desires. This means you can live your life united with Christ! It's not enough to quit the addiction; you must replace your dependency on it for a life of depending on *God*. He created you to be in an intimate relationship with Him, and nothing else will satisfy.

When you are at your weakest, God is at His strongest. When you need to escape, then escape into His presence. When you feel like giving in to your addiction, give into God instead. Utilize His wisdom and power found through the Bible and His Spirit. Bare your heart before Him, and use the mercy and power of His relationship to *beat addiction.*

Scriptures

The temptations in your life are no different from what others experience. And God is faithful. He will not allow the temptation to be more than you can stand. When you are tempted, he will show you a way out so that you can endure.

–1 CORINTHIANS 10:13 (NLT)

So submit to the authority of God. Resist the devil, stand firm against him and he will flee from you.

–JAMES 4:7 (AMP)

For we do not have a High Priest Who is unable to understand *and* sympathize *and* have a shared feeling with our weaknesses *and* infirmities *and* liability to the assaults of temptation, but One Who has been tempted in every respect as we are, yet without sinning. Let us then fearlessly *and* confidently *and* boldly draw near to the throne of grace (the throne of God's unmerited favor to us sinners), that we may receive mercy for our failures and find grace to help in good time for every need appropriate help and well-timed help, coming just when we need it.

–HEBREWS 4:15-16 (AMPC)

Speak these words over your life

I can do all things through Christ who strengthens me, and that includes beating addiction. Regardless of how I feel, how many times I have given into my addiction, or how long I've experienced failure in this area, I declare by faith I am free from this addiction. Though thoughts, feelings, and desires for the addiction may come, I will not give in because I am strong in the Lord and the power of His might. I am an overcomer, and addiction is just another thing that I overcome on my path to accomplishing my God-given destiny. My past is forgiven, my present is empowered by my union with Christ, and my future is bright with my promised destiny!

I Can Deal Wisely In My Affairs

The Bible says that wisdom is the principle thing, so go get it! God places getting wisdom as our top priority! When people hear the word "wisdom," often they picture an older individual with white hair sharing astonishing insight thanks to their many years of experience. Though there is truth in this picture, it can leave us with the connotation that wisdom can only be acquired through the passage of time. However, wisdom is not gained solely through personal experience or age but through an open heart and a listening ear. God even said,

"If any of you lacks wisdom, let him ask God, who gives generously to all without reproach, and it will be given him." James 1:5 (ESV)

Wisdom from our Father God is ready and available for us if we will just ask Him! This is one of the most underutilized gifts of Christianity; we think we are too busy and can't afford to take a break to read His Word and pray. The truth is, we can't afford *not* to! Sometimes the pressures of life force us into making rash, emotional, and irrational decisions instead of calm, well thought through decisions. It's wisdom to do your homework before deciding, to weigh the pro's and con's, and to seek the counsel of a trusted friend or a professional— but only *in addition to* and *not instead of* seeking guidance from God.

God poured His wisdom and insight into the Bible, yet too often we are praying for an answer from Heaven when we haven't spent the time to find out what He *already* told us to do in His Word. Read it, and learn from God's specific actions and the principles of His Word.

When it comes to a specific situation such as which school to attend, which career to pursue, who to marry, how to parent, what to buy, and where to invest, God will most often lead us through His peace. In Proverbs 3, it says all wisdom's ways are peace. God uses peace as our spiritual conscience or counselor. His Spirit guides us by it and lets us know what is safe and beneficial for us. When we feel that peace is missing, it shows us what is dangerous. So, pray and seek God, lean on His Spirit for help, and be sensitive to His peace in your life. Follow His wisdom, and you'll make good choices with wonderful outcomes.

Scriptures

But the wisdom that is from above is first pure, then peaceable, gentle, and easy to be intreated, full of mercy and good fruits, without partiality, and without hypocrisy.

–JAMES 3:17 (KJV)

If any of you lacks wisdom to guide him through a decision or circumstance, he is to ask of our benevolent God, who gives to everyone generously and without rebuke *or* blame, and it will be given to him.

–JAMES 1:5 (AMP)

My goal is that their hearts would be encouraged and united together in love so that they might have all the riches of assurance that come with understanding, so that they might have the knowledge of the secret plan of God, namely Christ. All the treasures of wisdom and knowledge are hidden in him.

–COLOSSIANS 2:2-3 (CEB)

Speak these words over your life

I know that God's Word guarantees that those who ask God for wisdom will be granted their request. So, I take this moment in time to pray: "Lord, I ask for wisdom concerning my affairs, and I thank you for direction, answers to questions, clarity, divine insights, supernatural ideas, and guidance in my day to day life to achieve the call you have placed upon my life. In the name of Jesus, Amen." Because God's wisdom is now operating in my life, I walk with divine clarity. I declare that I will be patient in distressing times, as I trust and lean on the Lord for His counsel and guidance with full assurance that His wisdom will come. I will not yield to anxiety when faced with difficult decisions; instead, I will lean on God and His wisdom on how to move forward.

I Can Do all Things Through Christ

You can do *all things* through *Christ* who strengthens you! Most Christians know this verse, but few have utilized the immeasurable power that is contained behind it. Most believers focus on the first part—"I can do all things" and when the going gets tough they forget the most important part— "through Christ who strengthens me." The Creator of every living thing is ready to infuse supernatural strength into your being—if you will only push past any doubt that your circumstances produce and rely on Him. Through Christ, you have the power to accomplish your purpose and strength to handle any storm that blows in your life. His strength, His joy, and His peace are *already yours*. But are you living that way?

We all face disappointments, challenges, and obstacles throughout our lives. Sometimes it is easier to switch into survival mode, where we are praying and believing God just to make it through the week or even the day. But God wants so much more than that for you! His desire is for you to get close to Him—so close that you tap into His strength and His stamina when yours begins to fail.

The closer you are to God and let Him into your life, the more He permeates it, filling every crack of weakness with His grace and strength. In Ephesians 6:10 (AMPC) it reads, *"In conclusion, be strong in the Lord **be empowered through your union with Him**; draw your strength from Him that strength which His boundless might provides."*

God wants us to lean on Him. He is our Father, and He did not design us to walk through life alone! He wants you to walk through life happy and fulfilled, completely void of fear, because you trust in Him completely. You are His child, and He wants to run this race of life together *with* you so that you cross the finish line together! When you talk to God in prayer, when you read His Word, and when you seek His will in your life, you are cultivating a relationship that transcends this life and will last all of eternity. You're planting seed in a relationship that will breathe purpose, strength, peace, and joy into your life now and forever. So don't doubt yourself for a second, because God doesn't. Instead, audaciously press forward in life with the spirit of a conqueror!

Scriptures

I can do all things which He has called me to do through Him who strengthens *and* empowers me to fulfill His purpose—I am self-sufficient in Christ's sufficiency; I am ready for anything and equal to anything through Him who infuses me with inner strength and confident peace.

—PHILIPPIANS 4:13 (AMP)

God can do anything, you know—far more than you could ever imagine or guess or request in your wildest dreams! He does it not by pushing us around but by working within us, his Spirit deeply and gently within us.

—EPHESIANS 3:20-21(MSG)

We pray that you may be strengthened *and* invigorated with all power, according to His glorious might, to attain every kind of endurance and patience with joy;

—COLOSSIANS 1:11 (AMP)

Speak these words over your life

I can do all things through Christ who strengthens *and* empowers me. I am self-sufficient in Christ's sufficiency; I am ready for anything and equal to anything through Him who infuses me with inner strength and confident peace. When I am weak in human strength, then am I truly strong, able, and powerful in divine strength. So, I will not falter on my convictions, and I will not let persecution cause me to draw back from the call of Christ upon my life, for I am strong in the Lord and in the power of His might. I will be successful in every endeavor because I am not alone; greater is He that is in me then he that is in the world.

I Can Live Confidently

Child of God, Ambassador of Christ, and Temple of the Holy Spirit—Jesus, through His redemption, separated you from your sin and bestowed these titles on you so that you can walk with unshakable confidence in a world of turmoil. Jesus said,

*"I have told you these things, so that in Me you may have perfect peace and **confidence**. In the world you have tribulation and trials and distress and frustration; but be of good cheer take courage; **be confident, certain, undaunted**! For I have overcome the world. I have deprived it of power to harm you and have conquered it for you." John 16:33 (AMPC)*

Many desire to be confident, to be bold, but they are afraid of failure and what may happen if they step out or stand up for their dreams and their God. You may have lost your confidence along the way due to your insecurities or failures, but if your confidence was based on your experiences, achievements, abilities or will power, it was doomed to be shattered from the start! As a

Christian, true confidence is based on the God of
the Bible and enters our lives through believing the
words written by our Father God. It develops faith
in us and a union with Christ that causes our confidence to soar. The Bible says Christ came to live in
you and placed a new identity upon you. This
means your confidence is due to an uncommon
trust in who God says you are, what God says you
have, and what God says you can do. There is no
need to be afraid, insecure, or timid because you
have Christ with you and His identity in you! You
are able to approach life with the assurance that
you have the God of Heaven's Armies as your ally!

Life is full of challenges, and more than likely
we will make mistakes along the way, but as children of God, they should not cause us to lose our
confidence. We have His strength to get up when
life knocks us down, dust off our clothes, remind
ourselves of who the Bible says we are and accept
God's grace! Ultimate failure is not getting
knocked down; it's staying down. But though you
may fall seven times, you will rise again, confident in who God is and that He will work even
this for your good.

Scriptures

I have told you these things, so that in Me you may have perfect peace *and* confidence. In the world you have tribulation *and* trials *and* distress *and* frustration; but be of good cheer take courage; be **confident**, certain, undaunted! For I have overcome the world. I have deprived it of power to harm you and have conquered it for you.

–JOHN 16:33 (AMPC)

Since we have such glorious hope (such joyful and **confident** expectation), we speak very freely *and* openly *and* fearlessly.

–2 CORINTHIANS 3:12 (AMPC)

Therefore my heart is glad and my glory my inner self rejoices; my body too shall rest *and* **confidently** dwell in safety,

–PSALMS 16:9 (AMPC)

Speak these words over your life

God has not given me a spirit of fear but power, love, and a sound mind. I am not timid or indecisive, and I do not fear what other people say or do. I do not fear what tomorrow holds or worry about how I will overcome the challenges of today, for the Greater One lives in me. I will not let criticisms and comments deter me from being bold. I declare that I am bold to speak my mind, to share my heart, and to profess my faith whenever it is necessary. God is the source of my confidence, and I am ready and willing for Him to speak His words through me whenever He requires it. I will not live out my days in quiet isolation; instead, I will live out my days with a confidence that cannot be stopped and a voice that cannot be silenced.

I Can Make a Difference

You do not need a stage, a crowd, or a mission field to make a difference. You don't need to have it all together, a million dollars in the bank, or a magnetic personality to make the world a better place.

Christians can underestimate the power of their influence. You come into contact with many people every day—clerks, servers, co-workers, friends, and of course your family. Each encounter you have with someone has the potential to have a positive impact on their life. To many people, you may be the only Bible that they will ever read and the only God they will ever see. There are people you can reach—acquaintances, friends, co-workers, family members—that the greatest preacher in the world will never reach. The Bible puts it like this:

"Don't begin by traveling to some far-off place to convert unbelievers. And don't try to be dramatic by tackling some public enemy. Go to the lost, confused people right here in the neighborhood." Matthew 10:5-6 (MSG)

Your encounter doesn't have to involve a grand gesture or sharing some profound truth. It's not preaching a sermon to everyone you talk to, either. A warm smile, a kind word, or a listening ear can make a powerful difference in someone's life. Whatever your small act of kindness may be, whether it's buying someone's meal or a cup of coffee or taking the time to simply ask how someone is doing and allowing yourself a few minutes to truly care about their answer, it is showing to them the love of God in a way that words can't. St. Augustine put it this way: "preach the gospel each and every day, and when necessary, use words."

However, when the situation calls for it, be bold with your faith. If you see someone in pain, ask if you can pray for them. Most people, even non-believers, will accept prayer if they are having a tough time. We have the cure for every suffering and the solution to every problem, and His name is Jesus! You can make a significant positive impact on those around you with a lot less effort than you think when you give God the opportunity to speak through you.

Scriptures

"Don't begin by traveling to some far-off place to convert unbelievers. And don't try to be dramatic by tackling some public enemy. Go to the lost, confused people right here in the neighborhood. Tell them that the kingdom is here. Bring health to the sick. Raise the dead. Touch the untouchables. Kick out the demons. You have been treated generously, so live generously."

–MATTHEW 10:5-8 (MSG)

Therefore, my beloved brethren, be firm (steadfast), immovable, always abounding in the work of the Lord always being superior, excelling, doing more than enough in the service of the Lord, knowing *and* being continually aware **that your labor in the Lord is not futile it is never wasted or to no purpose.**

–1 CORINTHIANS 15:58 (AMPC)

"Then these righteous ones will reply, 'Lord, when did we ever see you hungry and feed you? Or thirsty and give you something to drink? Or a stranger and show you hospitality? Or naked and give you clothing? When did we ever see you sick or in prison and visit you?' "And the King will say, **'I tell you the truth, when you did it to one of the least of these my brothers and sisters, you were doing it to me**!'

–MATTHEW 25:37-40 (NLT)

Speak these words over your life

I choose to make a difference in the lives of those that I come in contact with on a daily basis. I choose to let the love, light, and life of God shine through me today. I am sensitive to the needs of those around me, and I am determined to have a positive impact on their lives. I choose to be kind and considerate to my family, my friends, my co-workers, and everyone within my realm of influence. I refuse to ignore or be blind to the sufferings of those near me. I purpose in my heart to actively look for opportunities to inspire, influence, and impact the lives of those around me with Jesus' life-changing power.

I Can Fight

Life is a battle, and becoming a Christian equips you with the necessary weapons and armor to finally win instead of simply surviving. The Bible charges every believer to "Fight the good fight of faith." This is choosing to believe the promises of God above what anyone or any situation may convey to you. When this becomes your reality, then though the storms of life may rage and the waves of adversity may crash against you, you will remain solid as a rock, unmoved. You believe in a power greater than anything a storm could muster and a truth more sure than any foundation known to man: God and His Word!

So put your trust in God to see you through. Refuse to lay down and let the circumstances of life beat you down and rob you of your joy. Fight against the temptation to fear, worry, stress out, and doubt God's ability and willingness to take care of you. Courageously engage in combat with the various issues, imaginations, questions, and desires that arise in our minds by exposing them to the truth of God's Word and forcing them to conform to the Lordship of Jesus Christ. The Greater One is in you, Jesus is with you, God is *for* you, and you walk in the favor of God! The devil and all the powers of darkness are no match for you when you walk in that truth. You have the spirit of a conqueror in you—it's time to exercise it!

Read the Word of God, spend time in prayer, and speak His words aloud all day, but especially when you are tempted to doubt. Develop a spiritual resolve that won't crumble at the first sign of opposition. Develop a dogged determination to push through the obstacles and barriers that have been holding you back. Develop a spiritual fortitude that will carry you through any battle and on to victory.

Everything in this world seeks to pressure you and cause you to conform to its ideals and ways of living, but it is high time we as Christians start fighting back against the gross public display of debauchery and sin. So fight the good fight of faith with everything in you—fight against your own selfishness, against your own inadequacies, and against your weaknesses, knowing that when your strength begins to fail, God's strength will kick in!

Scriptures

Fight the good fight of the faith in the conflict with evil; take hold of the eternal life to which you were called, and for which you made the good confession of faith in the presence of many witnesses.

–1 TIMOTHY 6:12 (AMP)

For our struggle is not against flesh and blood contending only with physical opponents, but against the rulers, against the powers, against the world forces of this present darkness, against the spiritual *forces* of wickedness in the heavenly (supernatural) *places*.

–EPHESIANS 6:12 (AMP)

If your faith remains strong, even while surrounded by life's difficulties, you will continue to experience the untold blessings of God! True happiness comes as you pass the test with faith, and receive the victorious crown of life promised to every lover of God!

–JAMES 1:12 (TPT)

Speak these words over your life

I will fight the good fight of faith. I will not back down or be cowardly when faced with adverse circumstances. I will overcome the challenges and obstacles of this life with courage and confidence and the spirit of a conqueror. When the storms of life come, I will not allow myself to be overwhelmed by doubt and fear; instead, I will put my trust in God. God is on my side. I know that I am not fighting alone, and if God is for me then who can be against me? I will fight back against my own selfishness and weaknesses, and I will strive valiantly towards the purpose God has given me and to accomplish all that I have been tasked with.

I Can Enjoy Life

Life is meant to be an adventure we undertake, not an assignment we must endure! Jesus said that He came to the world so that we could have an *abundance of life*, with His peace navigating us through the dark places and His joy acting as our strength to push through the storm with a smile. Sadly, most are fighting to survive their lives instead of enjoying them. They believe the lie that their happiness—or lack thereof—is dependent upon their circumstances. If things are good, they are happy; if things are not good, then they are sad. This will cause them to be up one moment and down the next, happy one day and depressed the next. Our society has actually made it popular to be stressed, tired, and busy. This emotional roller-coaster lifestyle is a ride the world may ride, but believers can experience something different.

The truth is, we can choose to enjoy our life regardless of what we are experiencing.

It's not a matter of ignoring difficulties or faking happiness in the face of adversity. It's *choosing* happiness, it's *choosing* to base your joy, your security, and your peace on the solid foundation of the Word of God. It's choosing to remember all the benefits and blessings afforded to you as a child of God. It's choosing to cultivate a lifestyle of thanksgiving instead of complaining. It's resting in confident peace in the midst of trying times—because you have faith in your God!

There is no need to allow your circumstances to dictate your attitude or to let the pain of the past or the potential problems of the future rob you of the joy of today. It's time to enjoy your life, to live your life to the fullest with a spirit too close to God to be encumbered by negativity, doubt, and victim mentalities! Choose to smile right there in the middle of your messy life, walk on the bright side of the road, look up at the sky, trees, and birds, listen to fun music on the way to work or school, or watch something funny and laugh with the one you love. And when crisis strikes your life, like it does to all of us, stay full of joy and lean on God. Life was never meant to be endured but enjoyed.

Scriptures

You make known to me the path of life; in your presence there is fullness of joy; at your right hand are pleasures forevermore.

—Psalm 16:11 (ESV)

The thief comes only in order to steal and kill and destroy. I came that they may have *and* enjoy life, and have it in abundance to the full, till it overflows.

—John 10:10 (AMP)

Enjoy the Lord, and he will give what your heart asks.

—Psalm 37:4 (CEB)

Rejoice in the Lord always delight, gladden yourselves in Him; again I say, Rejoice!

—Philippians 4:4 (AMPC)

O taste and see that the Lord our God is good; how blessed fortunate, prosperous, and favored by God is the man who takes refuge in Him.

—Psalm 34:8 (AMP)

Speak these words over your life

I choose to be happy. I choose to base my joy, my security, and my peace on the solid foundation of the Word of God. This is the day that the Lord has made, and I will rejoice and make the choice to be glad in it! Even if this day presents adversity, challenges, and unwanted events, I will still choose to rejoice because I know that the Lord is with me. He encourages me, He supports me with His strong right arm, and He strengthens me. The joy of the Lord is my strength! I choose to cultivate a lifestyle of thanksgiving instead of complaining. I choose to trust that God has my back and to smile in the midst of trying times because I have faith in Him!

I will not allow my circumstances to dictate my attitude, and I will not allow the pain of the past or the potential problems of the future to rob me of the joy of today. I will enjoy my life. I will live my life to the fullest, because I am partaking of the abundant life Jesus came to give me. I reject negativity, doubt, and a victim mentality, and instead I choose joy!

I Can Forgive

Unforgiveness is a trap; it hinders our prayers, poisons our souls, and breeds bitterness. It casts shadows upon our otherwise happy lives. Your joy and peace begin to drain from your life. The sun doesn't shine as bright, flowers don't seem to hold the same beauty they once did, and the company you keep doesn't make you smile anymore when we do not forgive.

Unforgiveness is extremely toxic and wraps us up in bondage until we are controlled by our old memories instead of making any new ones. Many want to move on from the offense that was done to them or the mistakes that they made, yet the only way to truly move on is to forgive them or to forgive yourself. If you try to move on without forgiveness in your heart, then you will always be running away from your hurt, trying to create distance from your pain, but the problem is when we do not forgive, we have chosen to keep holding onto the poison that is killing us. However, the moment you choose to forgive those who have hurt you, you make the decision that allows you to deal with your pain instead of running from it. Now you can start living your life pursuing your God-given destiny!

It may seem impossible, it may feel like you'd be letting them win by forgiving, but with God's help you can traverse the bumpy terrain from a decision to true forgiveness. The first step is to spend time with God. God loves you, and when you spend time reading the Bible, praying, and worshiping God, He is able to pour His love into your heart. There is only so much room in your heart, and the more love He pours in, the more your shame and hatred begin to flow out. The second step is to pour out what God has poured in. You can't give what you don't have; many fall short and hold on to their bitterness and unforgiveness because they haven't received forgiveness or love on the level that they received hate and shame. However, after receiving God's love and forgiveness for you, you are able to replace your bitterness with love and forgive the unthinkable like God did for you. Then you get to start the cycle of love all over again, filling up on and pouring out God's love, instead of the cycle of pain you once prescribed to.

Scriptures

If we freely admit that we have sinned and confess our sins, He is faithful and just (true to His own nature and promises) and will forgive our sins dismiss our lawlessness and continuously cleanse us from all unrighteousness everything not in conformity to His will in purpose, thought, and action.

–1 JOHN 1:9 (AMPC)

But instead be kind and affectionate toward one another. Has God graciously forgiven you? Then graciously forgive one another in the depths of Christ's love.

–EPHESIANS 4:32 (TPT)

Judge not, and ye shall not be judged: condemn not, and ye shall not be condemned: forgive, and ye shall be forgiven:

–LUKE 6:37 (KJV)

Be gentle and forbearing with one another and, if one has a difference (a grievance or complaint) against another, readily pardoning each other; even as the Lord has freely forgiven you, so must you also forgive.

–COLOSSIANS 3:13 (AMPC)

Speak these words over your life

I am thankful that I have been forgiven. God, in His mercy and by His grace, has forgiven me of all my sins, mistakes, and shortcomings. I choose to accept God's forgiveness and His unconditional love. Even though I may not feel it, by faith I know that according to God's Word, I am righteous, in right standing with God, and He sees me as someone who has never sinned. It is by this state of righteousness bought by God's unconditional love through the shed blood of Jesus Christ that I am able to echo that same spirit of forgiveness and love to those around me. So, with the Lord's help and by the power of the Holy Spirit, I choose to wholly and completely forgive all of those who have hurt me, betrayed me, defamed my character, ignored me, or caused emotional or physical damage to me. By faith, I choose to let go of every one of those grudges and walk in the freedom that God paid for me.

I Can Rest

Life can get very tiresome—and not just physically. Trying to be the perfect spouse, parent, or employee causes a lot of mental and emotional wear and tear. We experience the pressure to conform to the expectations of others, to be a good friend, model citizen, dutiful churchgoer, or tireless volunteer—the list could go on and on. Each one of these things has the potential to produce worry, anxiety, and stress in our lives. As the years go on, as a society we keep looking in all the wrong places to get the rest we so desperately need. Our lives are getting busier and busier, but more caffeine and less sleep are not the solutions—nor are stress relieving scents, lotions, and oils the best way to cope. Obviously, being sleep deprived affects our performance and takes its toll on our health, but there is a greater threat that has crept into our society: a weariness of the soul. And this is the kind of tired you can't sleep off.

Walking through life when you are weary will cause you to go down a destructive path where you begin to hate what you once loved, and ultimately you will adopt a selfish and self-destructive behavior. Many of us settle just for a moment of "peace"—time away from it all—but the problem with this kind of momentary cease-fire is we come back to the same life we tried to escape.

Real rest comes from the Lord. He said it Himself in Matthew 11:28-30 (MSG): *"Are you tired? Worn out? Burned out on religion?* **Come to me. Get away with me and you'll recover your life. I'll show you how to take a real rest.** *Walk with me and work with me—watch how I do it. Learn the unforced rhythms of grace. I won't lay anything heavy or ill-fitting on you.* **Keep company with me and you'll learn to live freely and lightly."**

You see, the rest we are all seeking can only be found in Christ. Resting in the Lord is casting all the cares of your life on God—giving Him your troubles, your anxieties, your insecurities, your worries, and all your stress. Though, it's not enough to just cast the cares; it's up to us to leave those cares with Him by placing our complete confidence and trust in Him. Then we will be able to take a real rest, knowing we are in safe hands.

Scriptures

Come to Me, all you who labor and are heavy-laden *and* overburdened, and I will cause you to rest. I will ease and relieve and refresh your souls.

–MATTHEW 11:28 (AMPC)

But they that wait upon the Lord shall renew their strength; they shall mount up with wings as eagles; they shall run, and not be weary; and they shall walk, and not faint.

–ISAIAH 40:31 (KJV)

Casting the whole of your care all your anxieties, all your worries, all your concerns, once and for all on Him, for He cares for you affectionately *and* cares about you watchfully.

–1 PETER 5:7 (AMPC)

And he said, My presence shall go with thee, and I will give thee rest.

–EXODUS 33:14 (KJV)

The LORD is my shepherd. I lack nothing. He lets me rest in grassy meadows; he leads me to restful waters;

–PSALM 23:1-2 (CEB)

When you lie down, you shall not be afraid; yes, you shall lie down, and your sleep shall be sweet.

–PROVERBS 3:24 AMPC)

Speak these words over your life

Before He left this earth, Jesus said that He gave us His peace. He called it, "a peace that passes human understanding." By faith, I choose to receive that peace and step into the rest He offers me. I cast all my cares, worries, frustrations, and anxieties on Him. Even in the midst of the challenges, disappointments, and unexpected setbacks, even in the worst situations that life can offer, I make the choice here and now, I choose—and will always choose—to trust in God. According to His Word, I qualify to receive a supernatural rest that is only reserved for those who put their trust in the Lord. By faith, I take that rest. I know that the Lord will act as my refuge forever, sheltering me from the storm, providing a place of peace and an opportunity for rest with the promise that He will never leave me and will always be with me.

I Can Be Intimate With God

God loves you. You are His child, and He loves you unconditionally. He desires to spend time with you. Most people's concept of Christianity is that it is a religion with a long list of rules that they must obey in order to escape hell. It inaccurately paints God as an authoritarian tyrant and falsely describes the Christian life in terms of condemnation, fear, and penitence. They think it demands serving God out of duty and that your acceptance is based on your piety, holiness, and good deeds. However, this type of religious lifestyle makes for a fickle Christian walk, because it bases your sense of self-worth on what you do instead of what God has already done for you.

This is not the Christianity that Jesus died for us to gain!

Have you ever wondered why God created us? It was because He wanted children of His own! He even made us in His own image! So, when Adam and Eve messed up and cut humanity off from a relationship with God, God stopped at nothing to restore fellowship with His beloved children. He even gave up His son, Jesus, as a substitute for our sin to accomplish this goal. That's how much He desired to have a relationship with us. He was willing to watch His boy tortured and killed to give us the chance to run into His open arms. This is true Christianity—relationship. In a relationship, we serve out of love and loyalty, not fear and duty.

Like any relationship, developing this intimacy doesn't happen overnight; it takes time. The easiest way to start down the path of growing more intimate with God is simply by spending more time with Him. He said He would never leave you or forsake you, which means you can talk to Him as much as you want. You can read the Bible, gaining insight into the way God thinks, as well as hearing what pleases and displeases your Father. God will be as much a part—or as little of a part—of your life as you want Him to be. As you value His words, get to know Him, develop your faith in Him, and spend time talking to Him throughout your days, regardless of your circumstances. Then your relationship will grow, and an intimacy between you that is unique and special to both of you will develop. This is what Christianity is about—an intimate relationship with your Father God.

Yes, furthermore, I count everything as loss compared to the possession of the priceless privilege (the overwhelming preciousness, the surpassing worth, and supreme advantage) of knowing Christ Jesus my Lord *and* of progressively becoming more deeply *and* intimately acquainted with Him of perceiving and recognizing and understanding Him more fully and clearly. For His sake I have lost everything and consider it all to be mere rubbish (refuse, dregs), in order that I may win (gain) Christ (the Anointed One).

–Philippians 3:8 (AMPC)

In conclusion, be strong in the Lord **be empowered through your union with Him;** draw your strength from Him that strength which His boundless might provides.

–Ephesians 6:10 (AMPC)

"Have I not commanded you? Be strong and courageous! Do not be terrified or dismayed (intimidated), **for the Lord your God is with you wherever you go.**"

–Joshua 1:9 (AMP)

'Do not fear anything, for I am with you; Do not be afraid, for I am your God. I will strengthen you, be assured I will help you; I will certainly take hold of you with My righteous right hand a hand of justice, of power, of victory, of salvation.'

–Isaiah 41:10 (AMP)

Speak these words over your life

Today marks a new day in my relationship with God. I make the choice to prioritize God above everything else in my life. When I grow tired and weary, I will run to Him for rest. When I become stressed, worried, anxious, or afraid, I will cast my care upon Him, for I know how deeply He cares for me. I choose to keep God in the center of my life and in the forefront of my mind. My actions are out of a heart to please Him, and I will put to death my selfish and carnal nature daily. I choose to feed on God's Word, to spend time with Him in prayer, and go to Him first when I need help, instead of the last resort. I purpose in my heart to grow closer and more intimate with my Heavenly Father.

I Can Make It Through

No matter what you are going through, there are two things that are essential for you to remember: The first is that Jesus said that He would never leave you or forsake you. The second is that through faith in God—both in His Word and in His Spirit—you have the power, strength, fortitude, and resources to make it through any challenge, crisis, or difficulty you face. Sure, this life has difficulties and challenges, but we are never helpless, without support, or powerless. We can sail through the storms of life with an undaunted spirit. Jesus Himself said,

"I have told you these things, so that in Me you may have perfect peace and confidence. In the world you have tribulation and trials and distress and frustration; but be of good cheer take courage; be confident, certain, undaunted! For I have overcome the world. I have deprived it of power to harm you and have conquered it for you." John 16:33 (AMPC)

God knew you would experience problems; the fact that problems are in your life are not indicative of your shortcomings or a lack of faithfulness; nor are they a result of judgment on God's part. We live in a world in chaos, and problems come because of it. So, quit focusing on how or why the issue is in your life and start focusing on the solution to your problem: Jesus.

You see, the only way any situation can get the better of you is if you give it permission. Your peace, joy, attitude, faith, hope, character, and love are based on God, His Word, and His faithfulness, which are eternally stable and trustworthy. So no matter what situation comes your way—whether you messed up, it was an accident, or it was an attack—the bottom line is that God has provided the grace, strength, and guidance to make it through—and to be victorious! Sometimes it's easy to be overwhelmed when in the middle of a crisis—to let our emotions override our faith and dwell on the issue as if it wasn't already taken care of. But remember what Jesus said: you are not alone! Refocus your attention back on God instead of your problem by speaking His words, and your emotions will follow suit. You can and will make it through!

Scriptures

I've said these things to you so that you will have peace in me. In the world you have distress. But be encouraged! I have conquered the world."

—JOHN 16:33 (CEB)

Is anyone crying for help? GOD is listening, ready to rescue you. If your heart is broken, you'll find GOD right there; if you're kicked in the gut, he'll help you catch your breath. Disciples so often get into trouble; still, GOD is there every time.

—PSALMS 34:17-19 (MSG)

When I was desperate, I called out, and GOD got me out of a tight spot.

—PSALMS 34:6 (MSG)

Speak these words over your life

No matter what I am facing today, with the Lord's help, I can make it through. By the power of the Holy Spirit and the truth of God's Word, I will overcome. He sustains me, encourages me, strengthens me, and empowers me to overcome. Even if I get hedged in, pressed on every side, troubled, and oppressed in every way, I will not be crushed because greater is He that is in me than anyone else who could come against me. Even if I suffer embarrassments and am perplexed and feel unable to find a way out, I will not give in to despair because I know Jesus *always* makes a way out! Even if I am pursued, persecuted, and hard driven, I refuse to worry or be afraid because the Lord is with me, and He is always with me, upholding me. Even if I am knocked off my feet and struck down to the ground, I am not knocked out of the fight because my God is the God of hope, and as long as I don't give up and I cling to that everlasting hope that Christ provides, I cannot be destroyed.

I Can Speak Life

God spoke, and the world came into existence. He made us in His image, and our words are much more significant than many people have been led to believe. The Bible even says,

"Death and life are in the power of the tongue, and they who indulge in it shall eat the fruit of it for death or life." Proverbs 18:21 (AMPC)

Our words hold the power of life and death, and yet so many times, we let our mouth run wild instead of controlling the words that come out of it. Our words should not convey negativity and harsh criticism but rather minister life and hope to those who hear them. Many have believed the lie, "Live how you feel, say what you want." It sounds good, but its true deception lies in the fact that it only caters to one person: you. Following this philosophy will lead you down a road that eventually creates a self-centered critic that breeds negativity in your life and in the lives of those around you.

You shouldn't express every feeling or thought that comes to your mind; instead, you should examine your thoughts and filter them so that your words, even if they must convey constructive criticism or a harsh truth, will still leave the hearer uplifted, instead of downtrodden. The world is full of critics, but it is desperate for some encouragers! The Bible tells us that our words govern our direction in life. This means you have the capacity to change your situation regardless of what it may be! You never have to be a victim. You may have made mistakes that have put you in a bad spot. Though the world may have abused you in any number of ways, it's through God's Word that you can find forgiveness and healing, and confessing His Word with your mouth releases the life-shaping power that resides within your spirit. The Bible says God's Word is life! If you want to speak life over any situation, then find out what *God* has to say about it, and then speak it out loud with faith. Our mouths and minds should be filled with God's words, because then they will be filled with life. Speak God's Word over your life and with those you come in contact with. Speak life!

Scriptures

We are destroying sophisticated arguments and every exalted *and* proud thing that sets itself up against the true knowledge of God, **and *we are* taking every thought *and* purpose captive to the obedience of Christ,**

–2 Corinthians 10:5 (AMP)

A bit in the mouth of a horse controls the whole horse. A small rudder on a huge ship in the hands of a skilled captain sets a course in the face of the strongest winds. A word out of your mouth may seem of no account, but it can accomplish nearly anything—or destroy it!

–James 3:3-5 (MSG)

By faith that is, with an inherent trust and enduring confidence in the power, wisdom and goodness of God we understand that the worlds (universe, ages) were framed *and* created formed, put in order, and equipped for their intended purpose **by the word of God**, so that what is seen was not made out of things which are visible.

–Hebrews 11:3 (AMP)

Speak these words over your life

I speak life, health, healing, strength, and vitality to my body. I command my body to operate and function the way God intended it to. I speak peace, joy, supernatural intelligence, and understanding to my mind. I command my mind to be quick, sharp, witty, strong, at peace, full of joy, and alert. I have the mind of Christ and a body that will not hold me back from what God has called me to accomplish on this earth. I speak over my finances, and I declare that my debts are being reduced and eliminated. I claim the inheritance of abundance that He's given to me as His child. I have enough to accomplish all that I am called to do, with plenty left over for me to give and enjoy. I speak over every one of my relationships, and I declare that they be fruitful, that all bitterness and negativity must go, and to make way for love and peace. I call my family healthy, safe, and blessed. Finally, I declare that I will accomplish the purpose God has given me, I will be sensitive to the leading of the Holy Spirit, and I will enjoy a life full of all that God has given me.

I Can Be Led By The Holy Spirit

You can follow the Spirit of God. The Holy Spirit came to live and dwell in you when you accepted Jesus as your personal Lord and Savior. Many have been taught that the Holy Spirit is some fantastical being that is unpredictable and mysterious. However, the Bible clearly identifies who the Holy Spirit is and what He is here to do. He is our Helper, Counselor, and Teacher. He helps us understand the Scriptures and ultimately assists us in fulfilling God's plan for our lives, helping us navigate the tumultuous waters of life.

Though there are many ways He can lead us, there are two ways that He leads that are most common in our everyday life: through the Bible and through peace. The Holy Spirit always confirms the Bible, He will never contradict it. If you have a question of what to do, the first place you should always check is the Bible. The more you read the Word, the more you will be able to recognize the difference between your own thoughts and ideas and the promptings of the Holy Spirit. The Bible is inspired by the Holy Spirit and conveys God's thoughts to us. The more you listen to and read the way God thinks, the more you are able to recognize and then act on the thoughts and leadings He gives to you through His Spirit.

The second way He leads is by His peace. Pressures and worries come at us daily, but when we place our confident trust in God to help us, then He replaces our burdens with His peace. The Bible calls it "a peace that passes human understanding," and that is because it is a level of peace that doesn't make natural sense when you have problems all around you. It's through this state of being known as peace that we are able to discern where to go and what to do. Before making a decision, check your heart and see if you feel peace about doing it or if you feel an absence of peace concerning it. So, ask for the Holy Spirit's help, seek His counsel, fill up on the Bible, follow after His peace, and you'll find yourself right where you need to be—following the Holy Spirit.

Scriptures

For all who are led by the Spirit of God are children of God.

–ROMANS 8:14 (NLT)

And let the peace (soul harmony which comes) from Christ rule (act as umpire continually) in your hearts deciding and settling with finality all questions that arise in your minds, in that peaceful state to which as members of Christ's one body you were also called to live. And be thankful (appreciative), giving praise to God always.

–COLOSSIANS 3:15 (AMPC)

…What eye has not seen and ear has not heard and has not entered into the heart of man, all that God has prepared (made and keeps ready) for those who love Him who hold Him in affectionate reverence, promptly obeying Him and gratefully recognizing the benefits He has bestowed. Yet to us God has unveiled *and* revealed them by *and* through His Spirit, for the Holy Spirit searches diligently, exploring *and* examining everything, even sounding the profound and bottomless things of God the divine counsels and things hidden and beyond man's scrutiny.

–1 CORINTHIANS 2:9(B)-10 (AMPC)

Speak these words over your life

The Holy Spirit is with me. I choose to lean on Him as my teacher, my guide, and also as a very dear friend. I shall trust Him, and look to Him, to reveal the truth in God's Word, and the specific nature of God's plan and purpose for my life. I endeavor to grow closer and be more sensitive to the voice of the Holy Spirit so that He may lead, guide, and direct me in all things. With His help, I will be able to change and transform daily through the application of divine truths, insights, and revelations, and through the impartation of the Holy Spirit. In times of trouble, I choose to trust in God, and His Holy Spirit to warn me and guide me out. And finally, I choose to let the Holy Spirit shine through me producing goodness and mercy in my wake.

I Can Achieve My Dreams

Your life today is mostly the product of the decisions you have made in the past. This can be a sad reality for some who feel like failures, with their dreams unrealized and their goals unfulfilled. And if their story was to end today, it would be a tragedy indeed. But the good news is that this is not the end of your story. You are still writing your story with every decision you make. While you draw breath, there is hope for you and hope for your dreams.

Do not be discouraged if your life has not turned out the way that you thought, because just like your past has determined your present, your present determines your future! It's time to dream again! Change your future with the decisions you make—starting today! In the past, you may have tried to make it on your own merits and abilities, but now it's time to lean on God for support and guidance. It will take discipline—your dream won't just fall in your lap—but you have your Father God as a companion and the Holy Spirit as your guide to fulfill your destiny. The truth is, you are not the only one dreaming. You are God's kid, He has a dream for you too—to see you fulfilled, successful, with a wonderful family, and most importantly an intimate relationship with Himself.

God has a place where you will flourish, a job that He has grace for you to do, a family for you to cherish, and ultimately a disposition of joyful peace in all of your endeavors. It's not a fantasy; it's your reality! God never intended you to go into any venture or to undertake anything alone. Whatever it is, God wants to be a part of it, and He wants to help you in every area of your life. It doesn't matter how old you are or how many times you have failed, God is ready to help you achieve your goals and give shape to the dreams He's placed inside of you! Don't spend time dwelling on the impossibilities of what it will take; spend time meditating on how big and how good your Father God is! As you pray and seek God for your future, your first step towards your destiny is simple—love God and love others! As you keep these two directives as your guidelines for the decisions you make, you'll be on the right path towards your—and God's—dream for your life.

Scriptures

For with God nothing shall be impossible.

–LUKE 1:37 (KJV)

"For I know the plans I have for you," says the Lord. "They are plans for good and not for disaster, to give you a future and a hope."

–JEREMIAH 29:11 (NLT)

Roll your works upon the Lord commit and trust them wholly to Him; He will cause your thoughts to become agreeable to His will, and so shall your plans be established and succeed.

–PROVERBS 16:3 (AMPC)

For you have need of steadfast patience and endurance, so that you may perform and fully accomplish the will of God, and thus receive and carry away and enjoy to the full what is promised.

–HEBREWS 10:36 (AMPC)

Speak these words over your life

I declare that I will fulfill my God-given destiny. I will achieve the dreams and the goals that the Lord has given me. Even if I have been side-tracked or distracted, even if the mistakes and failures of my past have threatened to derail my future, even if I feel battered, beaten, and bruised with everything in me begging to throw in the towel and give up, even then, I will not concede defeat. These dreams I have are not just mine; they were placed inside me by God, and with His help, I will fight with all that I am to see those goals accomplished and dreams realized. And when my strength fades, I know I haven't even scratched the surface of the wealth and depth of God's immeasurable power He made available to me, His child. So, I boldly declare I can, and I *will*, achieve my dreams!

I Can Rise

The same Spirit that raised Christ from the dead lives in you! It doesn't matter how deep or how dark your pit may be; you do not have to be buried by your failures. Your shame and regret do not have to remain as a tomb for your ambitions, and your spirit does not have to be broken. That same unbreakable Spirit that ripped Christ out of the clutches of death and sin, causing Him to ascend on high, can also raise you out of whatever pit you find yourself in!

The time has come for you to RISE! *Rise* out of your bed of affliction. *Rise* out of depression and despair. *Rise* above the opinions of others. *Rise* out of the shame and regret of your failures. *Rise* out of mediocrity. *Rise* out of the sin that has ensnared you. It's time to base your identity on who *Christ* says you are instead of your past. It's time to throw off the weights that once held you, allow hope to rise within your heart, dare to dream, dare to discover, dare to overcome, dare to keep trying, and dare to act upon what you believe! You are a child of God, empowered and equipped with the mightiest weapon of all, faith in God! Your past cannot hold you any longer! Your *future* is bright because your *present* is filled with Christ! He was the first one to rise, and He's paved the way for each and every one of us to rise just as He did. God sent Jesus to pave the way, to give hope, and to restore His children to their rightful place as heirs to His kingdom.

The darkness can be familiar and seem inescapable, but you were made by and for the light. Don't allow your circumstances to shake you from believing the truth of God's Word. Even when the storm winds blow, hold fast to the words He has spoken to you and rise out of the pit by acting upon them! Jesus is your companion, your friend, your advocate, your help, and your support! If you slip, He'll catch you every time. If you get lost, He'll find you. If your strength fails, He'll carry you until you catch your breath. There is hope for you! There is freedom and joy in your future.

Scriptures

Arise from the depression and prostration in which circumstances have kept you—rise to a new life! Shine (be radiant with the glory of the Lord), for your light has come, and the glory of the Lord has risen upon you!

–ISAIAH 60:1 (AMPC)

for the light makes everything visible. This is why it is said, "Awake, O sleeper, **rise up** from the dead, and Christ will give you light."

–EPHESIANS 5:14 (NLT)

Yes, God raised Jesus to life! And since God's Spirit of Resurrection lives in you, he will also raise your dying body to life by the same Spirit that breathes life into you!

–ROMANS 8:11 (TPT)

Speak these words over your life

The same Spirit that raised Christ Jesus from the dead lives in me. That resurrection power gives me the strength, fortitude, and power to rise above anything that would try to hold me down and keep me from living life to the fullest measure. I dare to overcome. I dare to keep trying. I dare to act upon what I believe!

I will rise!

I will rise out of depression and despair. I will *rise* out of shame and regret. I will *rise* out of mediocrity. I will *rise* out of sin. I will *rise* above the opinions of others. I choose to base my identity on who Christ says I am. I'm throwing off the weights that once held me. I dare to dream. I dare to discover. I am a child of God, empowered and equipped with the mightiest weapon of all, faith in God! My past cannot hold me any longer! My future is bright because my present is filled with Christ!

About the Authors

Keith Provance, involved in Christian publishing for more than 40 years, is the founder and president of Word and Spirit Publishing, a company dedicated to the publishing and worldwide distribution of scriptural, life-changing books. He also works as a publishing consultant to national and international ministries. Keith continues to write with his wife and with his son Jake. He and his wife, Megan, have authored a number of bestselling books with total sales of over 2 million copies. They reside in Tulsa, Oklahoma and are the parents of three sons, Ryan, Garrett, and Jake.

You may contact Keith at
Keith@WordAndSpiritPublishing.com

Jake Provance is a successful young writer, who has written ten books and has plans to write several more. Jake's first book, Keep Calm & Trust God, has sold more than 700,000 copies. Jake is a graduate of Domata Bible School in Tulsa, OK, and has a call on his life to work in pastoral care ministry, with a particular passion to minister to young adults. Jake and his wife, Leah, live in Tulsa, OK.

You may contact Jake at
Jake@WordAndSpiritPublishing.com

Keep Calm & Trust God Vol 1
Issues such as anxiety, worry, fear, stress, setbacks, failures, etc. are addressed. Includes prayers, short narratives, scripture, poems and encouraging short stories – all directed to how to keep your cool and trust God.
$4.99

Keep Calm & Trust God Vol 2
Following in the footsteps of the best-seller Keep Calm and Trust God, volume 2 provides even more encouragement in love, hope, peace, joy, courage and faith. Includes prayers, short narratives, scripture poems and encouraging short stories.
$4.99

Keep Calm & Trust God Gift Edition
Bestsellers *Keep Calm and Trust God* and *Keep Calm and Trust God, Volume 2* are now combined together in a beautiful hardcover gift edition. It is arranged by topic to offer short stories, prayers, scripture and poems on whatever situation you may be facing. With an attractive cover, this edition is a welcome gift for friends and family.
$12.99

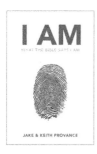

I AM What The Bible Says I AM
Presents seventeen chapters written to clearly reveal the truth of who we are. Each chapter is followed by scripture to take us to the Word and see what God has to say. Words of truth are included to reinforce the truth by speaking it. The perfect tool to discover the reality of who we are in Christ and walk in the fullness of the inheritance He has provided for us.
$4.99

I HAVE What The Bible Says I Have
Written to help new believers, and those who have been God's kids for a while, see the gifts and promises in God's Word and seeks to empower them to live the life God destined them to live. Clearly reveals the truth of what we have in Christ with scripture, and words of truth that can reinforce the truth by speaking it.
$4.99

I Can Do What The Bible Says I Can Do
Designed to offer inspiration and encouragement based on the truths in God's Word and the application of those truths into your life. Believers will be encouraged to overcome any challenge and enjoy victory in every area of life.
$4.99

Let Not Your Heart Be Troubled
Written to offer hope, encouragement and strength to a world that is under constant assault mentally, emotionally and physically. It is formatted topically to deal with issues such as loss, discouragement, and weariness. Scriptures, quotes, meditations and prayers are included to give answers to impossible questions of life and challenges that lie ahead.
$4.99

Scriptural Prayers for Victorious Living
This bountiful treasury of scripture based on prayer is a powerful tool designed to inspire and equip believers with the confidence needed to pray effectively and efficiently. It provides just the right words to pray scripture and stand on God's promises when faced with crisis, discouragement, fear, rejection, stress and anxiety.
$4.99

Jesus is King
Written to inspire and encourage us to live in the fullness of life that Jesus Christ provided for us. Every chapter brings understanding and clarity of who Jesus was, what Jesus did, and what He is still doing today! Provides a unique perspective by blending short narratives, scripture and inspired insights by Christian leaders. An extraordinary look at Jesus that will leave a powerful imprint.
$4.99

Coming soon:

Don't Quit
Burn the Ships